Overcoming Anxiety, Depression, Anger, Couple and Family Stress

KIRKUS REVIEW

This short, reflective guide to overcoming common relationship obstacles offers strategies for stronger communication and resolution.

Debut author Fowles doesn't fill her pages with anecdotes, tips, lists, and metaphors, as so many other self-improvement books tend to do. Instead, she offers a succinct, minimalist approach to handling issues such as anxiety and depression when they create dysfunction in family and couple relationships. The opening chapters offer insights into making certain one's "self" is honored in any relationship dynamic. She emphasizes the importance of saying "yes" only when one means "yes," and not when one simply wants to appease, avoid tension, or seek approval. She further expands the notion of honoring the self's desires with a chapter on quieting negative "voices"—beliefs formed in childhood regarding one's sense of self-worth and self-image. Although her anecdotes are few, they are powerful; for example, she offers an illustration of two different girls getting ready to go to the same birthday party. One's family members encourage, support, and praise her when she shows her new dress to them. The other's family puts her down, criticizes, and shames her. It becomes clear that the two girls will grow up with entirely different notions of self. Fowles expertly weaves this same idea into later chapters about couples and families, pointing out that these dynamics draw on past affirmations or degradations. One of the most valuable chapters teaches "passive listening," in which a listener supports someone by refraining from posing questions, imposing judgments, or giving extensive advice, in order to give the person space to arrive at his or her own realizations. This author also demonstrates this powerful tool through scripted examples.

An invaluable book about developing empathy in relationships and strengthening one's inner voice.

WRITER'S DIGEST

OVERCOMING ANXIETY, DEPRESSION, ANGER, COUPLE AND FAMILY STRESS by Judith B. Fowles, MA, LCPC is an excellent book for those seeking to understand themselves and others. Readers don't need to feel any of the emotions named in the title to benefit from this book. Written by an author who's qualified to tackle the subject, the material is conveyed in an easy to understand and relatable style. It was hard for me to put this book down. I realize that phrase usually refers to exciting novels, but this work is compelling enough to deserve this praise. Speaking of praise, I was surprised to find that praising others can block communication. But as the author explained, improper praise can hold people back. So false flattery and dishonest praise meant to make a person simply feel better doesn't help. That is only one interesting aspect of the book. First along, the author helps the reader learn how to communicate effectively, and to run from danger (for example, a romantic partner who's too jealous, etc.) This might seem like common sense but it's good to see because who knows -- someone vulnerable to abuse just might find life-saving help. Nice work. The cover is just okay, though the colors are nice. I appreciated the author's photo and bio on the back, and the copy made me want to read the book right away. I also enjoyed the personality analysis. This is an important book to refer to and simply to read any time.

Overcoming
Anxiety, Depression, Anger, Couple and Family Stress

Judith B. Fowles, MA, LCPC

A wholistic approach

This book is designed to present educational information only. The material included here should not be regarded, in any way, as a substitute for the mental health counseling provided by a qualified counselor. If mental health assistance is needed, seek the services of a professional in the field.

Designed by
Maine Authors Publishing
558 Main Street
Rockland, Maine
www.maineauthorspublishing.com

Produced by
CreateSpace

Printed in the United States of America.

To my clients

Contents

SECTION IV
The Family

SECTION V
Parenting

SECTION VI
Know Yourself

Introduction

O*vercoming* provides coping strategies that help you identify and move beyond ways of thinking that perpetuate distressing symptoms like anxiety, depression, anger, and other negative emotions. The book provides a cognitive behavioral approach to self-understanding. The cognitive behavioral perspective proposes that if you change how you think, you will change how you regard yourself and others, and how you react to what happens in the world.

The coping skills presented encourage a self-focused rather than reactive point of view. Self-focus is self-directed and leads you forward toward achieving what you want. A reactive perspective creates emotional upset and unwanted outcomes.

One way to understand the difference between self-focus and reactivity is to think of your life as a river you are born on. You are in a boat. If you live reactively, you are buffeted this way and that by the storms and turbulence on the river. You have little control over where you travel. If you conduct your life from a self-focused perspective with your authentic self at the helm, you steer the boat where you want to go despite the storms.

Overcoming presents a series of strategies and coping skills designed to:

1. Help you separate out who you are authentically and what you want to do from what the negative chatter in your mind and the critical people in your life say you should be and do.

2. Change your relationships with others from being difficult and distant to becoming stable and emotionally healthy.

3. Increase your self-understanding by discovering your personality type.

Overcoming is divided into six sections that present 33 coping skills. As a psychotherapist, when I'm seeing a client on a weekly basis, besides the other issues we address, I introduce one skill at a time. During the week, for homework, the client tries to incorporate that skill into daily life.

Section I explores strategies for overcoming ways of thinking and reacting that are problematic. The second section presents communication skills for improving relationships. Sections III and IV relate to problems that couples and families encounter. Section V addresses the challenges parents face. The last section presents personality typology theory and two reference chapters. The first reference chapter identifies and describes your personality type. The second shows how your type interacts with others. Learning about personality types provides a way to understand yourself and others better.

Overcoming is designed for the person who seeks better understanding of self and others, for the professional to use during therapy sessions, and for teaching psychological theory experientially to high school, college, and graduate school students.

I

Self-Focus
vs.
Reactivity

1 • Live in the Moment

We need the concept of time to be able to think and to orient ourselves in the present, but thoughts of the past and the future only exist in the mind. Often when depression or anxiety is a problem, one's thoughts are caught in either the past or the future. Many times thoughts of the past create depression and thoughts about the future bring on anxiety. A way to relieve these thoughts is to continually bring the focus of the mind into the present.

The body can only exist in the present and the mind can only think of one thing at a time. By bringing the mind back to where the body is, over and over, and by concentrating on what you are doing now, you can rest your mind from what makes you sad and what worries you. For instance, if you are folding the laundry, don't let your mind think about anything else. Think about how the laundry smells and feels. Watch your hands work. If it feels helpful, concentrate on folding the laundry well. Smooth the clothes. Make the corners fit together neatly. Relax. Do a good job so you will feel satisfied. If you are watching TV, only allow your mind to follow the program. When you notice your mind wandering, say "stop" to yourself and bring it back to the present, to where your body is (Millman 2005).

Of course, our ability to think about the past and future are crucial to our ability to function in the world. We build knowledge and skills, step by step. We need to be able to remember what we did yesterday and what our plans are for tomorrow and the future. We need to remember past mistakes in order to avoid them. We need to pay bills and fulfill future commitments, but when we're caught up in the past or the future with thoughts that go round and round (thoughts that hurt rather than help us), letting go of them and consciously willing ourselves to focus on *now* brings relief, frees the mind, and relaxes the body.

Think of life as a piece of film that unfolds frame by frame. If life has become overwhelming, stay in the frame you are in right now. Do the best you can right now. The past is gone. The future has not arrived. Neither exists except in your mind. If you have a bill that you can't pay, do your best to make plans to pay it. Once you have, let it go and deal with paying it when you have to, when you come to that frame, because something unexpected may happen and the problem may solve itself. This works with any problem you have. Do your best to take care of it now. Then stop worrying. Worrying is wasted energy which does nothing to help the problem. It only hurts you. By worrying about the future when we don't really know how it will turn out or by being sad about the past, we miss the good that is happening *now*.

Because of the way we have all been brought up in this culture, our minds default to the negative. We think about what we don't have, how we should look, what we should be doing, how we fall short, regrets, losses, and so forth. Turning off those thoughts and living in the now allows one to stop, look around, and think about what is working, what is okay—what we *do* have. Usually, when we can stay in the moment, we can say to ourselves, "I'm all right right now."

2 • Don't Say "Yes" When You Want to Say "No," Because Living Reactively Damages the Body and Mind

Living reactively means that what you do is mostly determined by outside influences; that is, you react to what others want you to do and try to adjust to their needs rather than your own. If you grew up in a family environment where emotional abuse (overly critical language and restrictive rules), neglect, or physical or sexual abuse was present, you learned to live from this reactive perspective. You learned that in order to gain acceptance or to protect yourself from hurt feelings and harm, doing what the other wanted you to do was the only way to cope. You learned that it was events and the people outside yourself that determined how things would turn out.

Even though this way of coping helped you survive emotionally as a child, it works against you now, and you need to unlearn it. Here is why:

You feel responsible for the happiness of others but not your own. You feel guilty and upset when others have problems and get overly involved with helping them. You do things for others that they could be doing for themselves. You feel safest when giving, because you feel guilty when others give to you. For that reason, other people seem to take advantage of you. You don't believe anyone could want you as you are, so you *do* for others to make them *need* you instead. You become hurt and angry when others don't support you the way you support them. No one is there for you. How can that be after all the sacrifices you've made for others? Finally, you don't really know who you are or what you want, and as time goes by you are getting madder and madder (Beattie 1987).

You have a critical judge inside you that makes you miserable. Its judgment turns inward upon you and outward toward others. Its point of view is negative. The harshness of this judge is ruled by how harshly you were treated as a child and is reinforced by how harshly you are being treated now. You may hear this voice as your own, but it is not. It is the voice of the critical or abusive other—your father, mother, spouse, friend, sibling, boss, or the critical voice of society. It is as if this *other* were living inside you, second-guessing you, putting you down, and attacking your self-esteem and confidence. It undermines, rather than supports you. You hear it rather than your own authentic voice, because instead of seeing and reacting to the world through your own eyes, you see everything from this other's (Ibid.). If the influence of this voice, rather than your own, is what controls you, then you do not own your own life and cannot determine your own future. If you cannot quiet this voice and your reactions to other negative outside influences, eventually you will become depressed, anxious, and feel like you are going crazy.

Everyone who has grown up in our culture is overly reactive to some degree. We default to negative thinking, because that is what most of us were brought up to do. We gained this perspective because bad behavior was punished and good behavior taken for granted. The emphasis was on the negative. A way to figure out how reactive you are is to pay attention to how many times you say "yes" when you want to say "no." If you are so confused that you don't know whether to say "yes" or "no," pay attention to what your body says. If you say "yes" and your body feels irritated, then you should have said "no." (There are some exceptions to this rule, which involve responsibilities that cannot be ignored.)

Aligning with your own authentic voice begins by asking yourself, "What do I want? Where do I want my life to go from here?" Often these are difficult questions to answer. Begin the process of understanding yourself by saying "yes" when you want to say "yes" and "no" when you want to say "no."

Think of emotions as the body's energy. Anger, anxiety, sadness, happiness, love—all the emotions—are experienced in the body as different kinds of energy. Each emotional energy impacts upon the body and mind with a different feeling. When disturbing emotional energy enters the body, it gets stuck in various places—the stomach, the heart, the bowels, the head, the muscles of the neck and shoulders. Think for a moment how the emotional energy of anger feels and where it hits you in your body when you get angry. How are the emotional energies of anxiety and sadness experienced differently? Where do you feel those emotions in your body?

Each time you say "yes" when you want to say "no," you hurt your body someplace, because you feel angry or irritated or sad when you do it. After this happens over and over, the immune system breaks down and illness develops in those parts of the body that have been impacted—the stomach, the colon, the muscles and tissue, the heart. Acid reflux, Crohn's disease, heart disease, and fibromyalgia are common conditions that develop from years of this kind of stress on the body. To avoid this damage, move disturbing emotional energy through your body and out of it as fast as you can, or keep it from getting stuck somewhere in the first place by using a coping skill like not saying "yes" when you want to say "no."

3 • Gain a Self-Focused Perspective

When a person has self-focus, he or she can set an intention to do something and move forward toward achieving it. Reaching the goal may be difficult, but the criticism and unreasonable demands of others do not sway that person from the path, nor do unanticipated events that block the way. Guilt, fear, lack of money, and physical problems are all hurdles that must be overcome, but the person has the self-focus, understanding, and determination to believe that, "If I do this, this and this, I will reach my goal."

For someone who has come from an emotionally or physically abusive environment, finding the way is a much more complicated and difficult task, because outside influences and the voice of the inner critic block the voice of the authentic self, and seem like too much to overcome.

Two Little Dancing Girls

Two little four-year-old girls, of equal intelligence and ability, have been invited to a birthday party. The first little girl, Jessica, was born into a home where her parents welcomed her. They were in their mid-twenties when she was born and had waited until they felt comfortable with themselves and were financially secure before planning to have a child. During the pregnancy, Jessica's mother read many books about taking care of herself and her baby while pregnant, and later she read books about how babies and children develop. After Jessica was born, her mother stayed home to take care of her, rocking her and singing her lullabies. Jessica's needs were met emotionally and physically. As she grew older, her behavior was guided in appropriate ways when needed by a firm voice or a time out for unacceptable behavior. Her parents never said anything mean to Jessica that would make her feel bad about herself or erode her confidence and self-esteem.

The second little girl, Emily, was born into a household where chaos reigned. Her father drank all the time and was often absent from the household. When he worked, he kept most of the money for himself. Her mother, at twenty-one, already had two other children and was worn out, impatient, and resentful that she had to stay home with kids while her friends were free to do what they wanted. When Emily's father came home drunk, he sometimes hit her mother. When she was little, her mother didn't always feed her or change her when she needed it. As Emily grew older, she was yelled at, called "stupid," and sometimes hit.

When the party invitation came through the mail to the first little girl's house, her mother planned an afternoon to take Jessica shopping for a party dress. They found a beautiful dress. When she got home, she was so excited that she ran into her bedroom and put on the dress.

Jessica's father, brother, and grandmother were sitting in the living room. Jessica ran in wearing her dress and twirled and danced around. Everybody clapped and said, "Jessica, you look so beautiful!" Jessica felt like a princess.

When the invitation arrived at Emily's house, her mother also decided to buy a party dress for her daughter. This was such an unexpected, exciting event that Emily was thrilled. She and her mother went to the store and found a beautiful dress. When they came home, she ran into the bedroom and put it on.

Emily's father, brother, and grandmother were sitting in the living room. Emily ran in wearing her dress and twirled and danced around. Her grandmother said sternly, "What's the matter with you! You're showing everyone your underwear. Nice little girls don't do that." Emily's joy disappeared in a flash. She felt confused and ashamed. She ran from the room crying.

In the first case, when Jessica felt beautiful and proud of herself, her sense of self was validated by others. What she felt on the inside was reflected back to her from the outside. Her self-esteem and confidence were reinforced. In the second case, when Emily felt beautiful and proud of herself, she was shamed. Her self-esteem and confidence were devastated. Her sense of self fractured.

With each day that passes in these two children's lives, the building blocks that will form their adult beliefs about themselves and the world are being established. As adults, they will move through life and make decisions for themselves based on these beliefs.

When Jessica goes to school, she will go well fed, rested, and dressed in appropriate clothes, knowing all is well at home. Because of that, she will be able to learn. For Emily it will probably be a different story. Perhaps she won't get supper every night. Her clothes may be soiled and mismatched. Her parents may fight at night, keeping Emily afraid and awake. At school she may worry about what will happen to her when she gets home or whether other kids will tease her on the way. Because of her anxiety, she will not be able to focus and learn. Maybe she will be diagnosed with a learning disorder and go through school labeled with it. All this will be difficult for Emily to overcome. As an adult, she will probably be anxious and depressed.

Of these two little dancing girls, which one represents you most? How much of what you do and believe is influenced by either your critical inner voice or the critical judgments of others?

4 • Quiet the Negative, Fearful, Worrying Voice

Because of their interactions with others as they were growing up, Jessica and Emily have opposite beliefs about themselves. Jessica is confident. Emily is not. Yet, they were born with the same abilities. The way they perform in life is only based upon the beliefs that were instilled in them, not on the reality of their abilities. And beliefs can be fleeting, because they are not solid like a chair. They are just thoughts, so they can change. To gain a better, more realistic perception of herself, her abilities, and what is possible for her to achieve in the world, Emily must change her belief system. This is a huge challenge. She must get rid of her critical grandmother's voice (and the voices of all the others who hurt her) and replace it with a more positive one—her own.

When you interact with the outer world from a self-focused perspective, you line up what the inner self wants to what happens in the outer world. This inner self is the *I* that lives in the body and looks out through the eyes. It is the authentic *you*.

Every self is unique and yearns to become itself in the outer world. When this self is stifled and the life one lives on the outside is too far from who one is on the inside, eventually the person becomes depressed without really knowing why, or anxious or very angry. Emotions like anxiety and depression are actually messages from the self that all is not well. The question for the individual to answer then becomes, "How can I change the way I think or the circumstances of my life so I can get rid of these awful feelings?" Being overly reactive to negative outside influences or being controlled by the inner critic keeps you from connecting to the authentic self; indeed, it keeps you from even knowing it is there trying to deliver a message.

The first step to connecting with the self is to say "yes" when you want to say "yes" and "no" when you want to say "no." The second is to change the way you talk to yourself, from a negative (unsupportive) way to a positive (supportive) way.

We are accustomed to letting our minds react on their own, especially when we are emotionally upset. Depending upon how the voice inside our minds directs us, we either speak to ourselves in ways that get us more upset or in ways that calm us down.

Lynn Clark, Ph.D., writes in *SOS: Help for Emotions*, "Our emotional upsetness is caused largely, but not entirely, by our beliefs and silent self-talk statements about events and situations, rather than by the actual events themselves" (p. 23).

In other words, it is not the disturbing event that creates the emotional upsetness, but the mind's reaction to it. Clark also says:

> Individuals continually engage in inner speech, internal dialogue, automatic sentences, or self-talk with themselves. These self-talk statements are nearly automatic and are at a low level of awareness. With this internal dialogue, we debate different courses of possible action and determine our feelings and emotional reactions to events and situations (Ibid.).

Clark identifies the process of how the reaction unfolds as the "ABC's of our Thinking, Feeling, and Behaving."

A = Activating Event

Clark calls disturbing events "activating events," because they get our emotions stirred up and we become reactive. We assume that the upsetting event causes the problem, but the upsetness is actually caused by our emotional response to the event. Clark points out that activating events can trigger emotional response on three levels—the past, the present, and the future.

Imagine that during their lives, Jessica and Emily have a similar experience when each is driving along a turnpike to a job interview—a tire goes flat and they swerve. They lose control briefly, then bring the car to a stop along the side of the road. Both experience upset, the pounding of the heart and fear, but Jessica can calm herself down. She thinks to herself, "Thank God I'm all right and the car is okay. I can handle this. I'll get through it. If I miss the interview, I'll call and explain what happened or I'll apply for another job." She sits and waits for a state trooper to come along and help her.

Emily overreacts. "Oh, my God! I almost got killed! What am I going to do? I can't change a tire! What if I get out of the car? Someone might come along and kill me or a car will hit me. But I have to get going. I'm going to miss the interview. This kind of thing happens to me all the time. It's not fair!"

Jessica remains calm, because she has the confidence to move through life based on her experience that things usually work out. Emily gets very upset and has little confidence, because her past experience leads her to believe that things usually don't work out.

The activating event of getting a flat tire impacted on Jessica and Emily emotionally at the three levels: their past good and bad experiences, their reactions in the present to the event itself, and their future concerns about the job interview. The amount of anxiety and anger generated by the experience was directly related to their beliefs.

B = Beliefs and Self-Talk

Clark writes, "B's are our beliefs and self-talk statements, what we tell ourselves about activating events" (p. 23). He labels these beliefs as either rational or irrational:

> Rational beliefs and self talk are self-helping, coping and adaptive statements that lead to emotional growth...Rational beliefs lead to less disturbed emotions such as concern, displeasure, annoyance, and sadness. Also, rational beliefs help us to cope more effectively, to get more of what we want out of life and to gain more contentment. The language of rational beliefs and self-talk is usually cool or warm in emotional tone, rather than hot or volatile (Ibid.).

Jessica calmed herself with rational self-talk. Clark states that "irrational beliefs [mistaken ideas] are self-harming, self-defeating, maladaptive, internal statements which lead to emotional upsetness...Irrational beliefs lead to anxiety, anger, depression, and to a feeling of not being in control of our emotions" (Ibid). Emily's irrational self-talk escalated her anxiety.

C = Emotional and Behavioral Consequences

The emotional consequences that result from irrational self-talk include out-of-control anxiety, anger, and depression. Negative behaviors that can result from becoming the victim of these emotions include staying at home, because you're afraid to go out (anxiety), being verbally abusive or hurting someone physically (anger), or staying in bed sleeping all day (depression).

The beliefs and self-talk we use to guide ourselves are instilled during childhood and through our interactions with others as adults. When your self, as a child or adult, has been positively validated, you will positively validate yourself. When your self has been criticized or abused, you will be self-critical and feel afraid and guilty. For the validated self, the world is a relatively safe place; for the invalidated self, it is not.

A Reality Window

With your imagination, create a window to look through. On the other side of the window is your life. What does it look like? Are you happy with it? Is what happens in your life based on what you want? Are the things you do and experience the result of rational or irrational beliefs?

The window can be changed. You can create a new reality window. Changing your reality window from an unhappy one to a happy one can be accomplished by changing what you believe to be true.

Reality is what we believe it is, as individuals and collectively. When we are born, we are born into a belief system—what our parents, neighbors, friends, television, newspapers, and the internet tell us the world is about. Generation after generation passes information on to their children, based on what was taught to them.

For instance, does anyone believe that a pile of paper with numbers on it is materially worth the same as a car? No. If that were the case, we would put numbers on pieces of paper and buy cars with them. What creates the value of money is our collective belief in its worth. The power of belief is enormous. Changing one's beliefs will change one's life. The process begins by becoming conscious of which of your beliefs are irrational and destructive and getting rid of them. Change the automatic irrational reactions of your mind to consciously thought-out, self-directed ones by changing the way you talk to yourself.

5 • Overcome Projection:
Become Conscious of How the Psychological
Phenomenon of Projection Influences How You Feel
and What You Do

Projection affects all of us every day. Like the old-fashioned movie projector, we project our own emotions and experiences onto others and situations. The projection causes us to misinterpret what is going on inside another, to overreact to what another does, and to overreact to events and circumstances that are like those that hurt, frightened, or stressed us in the past, especially in childhood. The reactive response is unconscious. Until you become conscious of how projection affects your life, you are caught in a trap of experiencing fear, jealousy, anxiety, explosive anger, panic, or sorrow over and over. Sometimes the emotions are felt very intensely, whooshing through the body. They become overwhelming so quickly that you can lose control and do something that brings on dire consequences.

Something important to know about projection is that the reaction and the point where emotional control is lost is not so much in the mind as it is in the body. Here is how it works:

A little boy, Mike, lives in a household where people are mean. Sometimes he watches his father hit his mother and cannot stop him. He is also hit, called names, and put in a dark closet for hours for punishment. While he is growing up, Mike is powerless, afraid, and angry.

Twenty-five years later, Mike is driving down the road when someone cuts him off. At this point, the emotion of anger starts to enter his body. As the energy of the anger is felt, his body remembers the feeling of rage that was in the immature emotional system of the helpless child, and whoosh, it ignites the man. He becomes overwhelmed and out of control. His mind cannot contain his anger, because the feelings are too huge and immaturely developed (at the level of a child). He chases the person down the road and starts bumping at the rear of the car and an accident occurs. Sometimes when someone is in this kind of rage, he or she won't remember what happened.

To a lesser degree, each of us has our own set of circumstances that trigger reactions to projective experiences. Overcoming the unconscious way projection affects our lives is difficult, because the response is ingrained and automatic. The reaction is created at the core level of personality, and disarming it cannot occur until you become aware of it.

When strong emotions overtake you, projection is usually at work. Like a movie camera, you are projecting something from the past onto the present circumstances and creating an inappropriate overreaction. This is usually true when you become very upset, except when something very upsetting is actually happening to you or someone you love, or some other event actually justifies the reaction. When you become highly emotional and reactive about something, ask yourself, "What is this really about? Am I being reasonable here or am I projecting something from the past onto the present situation?"

6 • Detach

Detachment is the ability to step outside a situation with your mind to perceive what is going on from a neutral, nonjudgmental perspective. The goal is to become a detached observer of the situation rather than a reactive participant.

The concept of detachment recognizes that, usually, we can't change another's thinking or behavior by arguing with words that seek to convince. We can't change another's behavior by trying to please the other in an attempt to control his or her moods and reactions. Detachment is also based on the reality that, even when we try, we can't solve another's problems. Ultimately, we must all solve our own problems. And by working to solve our own problems, we grow intellectually, emotionally, and spiritually; our mental health improves. When you try to solve another's problem, you deprive that person of the opportunity to find his or her own way to the solution.

Say you are having a dispute with someone. The goal of detachment is to remain reasonably calm, composed, and self-focused, even if the other person is angry and being verbally abusive. You may think you have to react in such a situation, but you don't. Instead of reacting automatically with words that reflect the first emotions that overtake you—anger, fear, hurt and the need to strike back, you can hold on. You can give yourself time to think about what to do from a self-focused perspective.

Detachment embraces the perspective that it is our reactions to events, rather than the events themselves, that cause problems. Therefore, blaming another or making the other person wrong (reactive responses) escalates upset and does not get you anywhere. Since you seldom change another's thinking and behavior through arguing or trying to please, and since blaming and making the other person wrong get you nowhere, there is only one thing left to do. Change yourself. All this makes a remarkable fact true: When you are taking care of yourself, you are taking care of everyone else and things fall into place.

Detachment involves getting reactive responses under control by using the previously mentioned coping skills: staying in the moment, gaining self-focus, supporting yourself with positive self-talk, and overcoming projection. Detachment cannot happen if you remain emotionally charged by the situation. Think of it this way: Imagine there is an emotional cord that links your reactions to another's words and behavior. Because of the link, he or she triggers your anger, distress, fear, worry, or sadness—reactive responses. By working at it, you can cut the cord that links you to the other person, thus detaching from the emotionally charged reaction.

7 • Self-Focus and Boundaries

Healthy psychological self-care requires that you create strong boundaries around interactions with others and the choices you make. The boundaries are set internally at first, through self-focus, then applied to the outside world. One way to begin setting appropriate boundaries is to start saying "yes" when you *want* to say "yes" and "no" when you *want* to say "no." Using this skill keeps others from taking advantage of you and allows you to get up in the morning with your own plans for the day, rather than those imposed by others. Over time, symptoms of anger, resentment, anxiety, and depression start going away, psychological health improves, and you become happier.

Setting a boundary is like building an invisible fence around yourself that keeps unwanted, unhealthy, emotionally disturbing psychological circumstances away. You bar them from your life as much as possible. Sometimes you have to do something drastic to make this happen—end a relationship, quit your job, get a divorce—but if you learn to set boundaries, maybe you won't have to take such drastic action.

Setting boundaries is difficult and uncomfortable, because it produces feelings of guilt and fear at first. Learning to tolerate the discomfort of these feelings is part of the process of learning to hold boundaries. To become successful and move beyond guilt and fear, you must come to understand and accept that it is okay for another to be angry with you when you do not do what he or she wants. Others are entitled to their feelings. When this happens, detach. Hold yourself together. Once you can hold boundaries consistently, remarkable results can occur—relationships improve, the job works out, the marriage is saved.

Say you are married to a man or woman who wants to control what you do, what you say, and with whom you spend time. I'm sure you've tried to change how this person treats you by arguing or by adjusting your behavior to please him or her in order to avoid arguments. Neither of these strategies will work. The person does not change. You remain angry. Over time, resentment and bitterness set in. The relationship deteriorates. Still, you put up with the behavior, walking on eggshells, hoping things will get better. This is futile because, actually, the only way you have to discover whether this person can change is to not put up with the behavior. To do that, you must get control of your reactive responses, gain self-focus, set boundaries, and follow through.

8 • Determine Who Owns the Problem

The first step in setting boundaries requires that you detach to gain a neutral nonreactive response to the situation. The second step is to determine who owns what problem.

For example, imagine that Emily (who grew up in an abusive environment) is now in relationship with a man, John. She has two teenage children from a previous marriage, Bobby and Mary. The four of them are living together trying to make things work. John is very critical of the children. Bobby and Mary bicker and fight all the time. They are noisy. They don't put things away. They are disrespectful. Their rooms are a mess. They don't help around the house. Bobby and Mary are teenagers, a trial to anyone living with them.

The children are resentful of John and will not cooperate. They become more and more distant, sullen. The house is full of tension. Emily is caught in the middle and tries to please everyone. She is exhausted mentally, emotionally, and physically. It seems that no matter what she does, nothing works. Everyone is angry. Her children's needs are not being met. John's needs are not being met. Her needs are not being met.

Although it may seem that if she just tries harder, she can make the problems go away, this is not the case. The reality is that she cannot solve her partner's problems with her children. She cannot solve her children's problems with her partner. The only problems she can solve are her own.

In this example, Emily is caught in the middle between her partner and her children. Her dilemma is that she is stuck in a triangle. Triangles are always difficult. If she sides with John when she thinks her children are being unreasonable, her children will get angry. If she sides with Bobby and Mary when she thinks John is being unreasonable, he will get angry. She can't win.

In order to determine whether the family can become a viable working unit, she has to extricate herself from the triangle and begin setting boundaries around what she will and will not tolerate and what she will and will not do. Her decisions need to be based on how she can best take care of her own mental, physical, and emotional needs in the situation (self-focus). Her point of view and decision-making process will be most effective if she can define what she *wants*. By removing herself from the reactive position in the middle, the place where she tries to please everyone except herself, she can detach and gain self-focus. Once she has, she can begin setting boundaries by saying "yes" or "no" and following through.

If you are living in a household like this, sorting through saying "yes" or "no" can be difficult. The relationships are complex. In a situation like this, the issues seem overwhelming and impossible to prioritize. Start by making a list of each person's unacceptable behavior. This list needs to be based on how *you* feel, no one else. Choose the issue you want to work on first; then start saying "no."

In this example, Emily contributes to the family's dysfunction and her own unhappiness by trying to please everyone else rather than herself. This problem is her responsibility to resolve. She owns it.

9 • Establish a Boundary

When someone wants you to do something and you say "no," you solve your own problem, but usually create a problem for someone else. Because this happens when you say "no," it may challenge your ability to hold the boundary, because feelings of guilt and fear set in. After all, your usual method of operating is to solve others' problems, not create them. When you set a boundary, though, the emotions of guilt and fear that upset you are obstacles to be overcome if you are to be successful at holding the boundary. If you give in to the feelings, you become reactive, lose self-focus and your state of detachment. When this happens, you will probably give in to the other's resistance to "no," and the boundary will crumble.

For instance, Emily, who is living with her boyfriend and two teenage children, needs to find a way out of the triangle she is caught in between them. Once she comes to understand this, she can begin to detach and become an observer of the family dynamics, rather than a reactive participant.

She begins to sort out the issues, to make lists to determine what her boyfriend does to upset her, what her children do. She tunes in to her feelings of annoyance, frustration, anger, and resentment, and pays attention to how many times she says "yes" when she wants to say "no." She must also focus on her own projection issues. For example, does she overreact when her boyfriend is upset and critical of her and the children because she was made to feel bad about herself as a child when she was criticized? She needs to figure out what emotional situations in her life now make her feel like she did then. When exactly does the present behavior of others trigger past trauma, causing her to feel as hopeless and helpless as she did as a child? We all have projective responses to work through. Emily must get in touch with hers to become conscious of her issues. She has to detach from their emotional impact so she can move forward. Once she does, she can decide what family issue she wants to address first; then she can come up with a plan and begin to implement it.

After thinking it through, Emily decides that the issue she wants to address first is John's criticism of the children's behavior. She decides that the boundary she will set is, "I will no longer listen and respond to his complaints when he is angry, being mean, or attacking the esteem of myself or the children." To successfully follow through, Emily has to formulate and establish this boundary securely within herself. Once this is achieved, she can express the boundary to John and mean it. She can also find the courage and resolve to stand fast when she starts feeling guilty and fearful as he resists her boundary. He may become very angry and emotionally abusive. (If you are living with someone who is also physically abusive, setting boundaries may put you in danger. Don't do it. Instead, seek professional help.) John may threaten to leave because now *he* has a problem; in order for his opinions to be considered, he has to find a new way to communicate them. He is being pressured to change, and he may not want to do that.

The boundary that Emily has established here addresses the problem she and John have communicating. It does not address the specific issues between John and herself or John and the children. Instead, it only deals with *how* they communicate. To successfully hold the boundary, Emily needs to stay focused on the boundary goal—improved communication. She wants to shift their communication style from being destructive and going nowhere to becoming constructive and making progress. Therefore, she needs to avoid conversations about the children's specific behavior and stay focused on the communication problem and her own self-focused perspective by repeatedly saying to John in different ways, "I understand you are angry and frustrated, but I get too upset when we argue this way. Until we can communicate in a more positive way, I'm not going to discuss the children's behavior at all."

10 • Create a Self-Focused Mantra that Will Keep You on Track

The word mantra is most commonly associated with meditation. It is a word or phrase that is used during meditation to keep one focused. Mantra actually translates into "thinker" or "to think." When you are setting a boundary with someone, often it is difficult to think clearly or stay focused because emotions take over. Creating a mantra for yourself that clearly states the boundary and memorizing it before you set the boundary can help keep emotional reactivity in check, aid in maintaining self-focus, and help you stay on track.

When you set a boundary with someone, the tendency is for that person to resist, become angry, and to argue with you about the boundary you have set. *You do not want to become involved in an argument with the other about who is right and who is wrong* after you have set the boundary. If you start trying to justify your position or attempt to prove the other person wrong, you will lose self-focus and become reactive. Once you become reactive, all is lost. The boundary-setting process will fail.

A mantra that is used to hold a boundary is a nonreactive response presented from a self-focused perspective. The purpose of using the mantra is to keep you focused on the boundary goal. An effective mantra that will help you maintain self-focus has two parts. First, it acknowledges and validates the other's feelings. This is always a good thing to do when you have a conflict with someone. The validation acknowledges the other's point of view and reduces the tendency for him or her to strike back. Secondly, the mantra states the boundary from the self-focused *I* position. It does not judge the other or make the other wrong. It simply describes how you are feeling and why you are setting the limit. The mantra, except for validating the other's emotional state, is only about you and your experience in the situation.

For instance, Emily has decided that she will no longer discuss the children's behavior with her boyfriend when he is angry, being mean, or verbally attacking her or the children. She needs to establish this boundary firmly within her before she presents it to John. A way to firmly establish this goal within her is to write it down and memorize it. Then, when he becomes angry about the boundary she has set, triggering her own emotional reaction, instead of responding reactively, she can fall back on the prepared self-focused mantra and stay on track. John needs to have his feelings validated, though, so the mantra she creates for herself should look something like this: "I understand that you are angry and frustrated about how the children act, but I get too upset when we argue this way. Until we can find a calmer way to talk about this, I'm not going to discuss the children's behavior at all."

As John continues to argue and resist her boundary, she can vary the response, but the content should remain the same; that is, she will say the same thing in different ways. For example: "You get angry. I know that, but the arguing gets us nowhere, and it upsets me too much. We need to find a better way to communicate" or "I understand that the children are driving you crazy, but arguing this way does not help, and I can't stand it. We need to find another way to deal with the problem."

II

Self
and
Others

11 • Become Aware of How You Communicate

As has been stressed in previous coping skills, how you speak to yourself within your mind (in a positive or negative, supportive or unsupportive voice) influences how you think, respond, and feel emotionally and physically. Just as you affect yourself through self-talk, you affect others by the way you talk to them. No matter what the issue, how you listen to another's point of view and how you respond to what is being said profoundly influences how things turn out.

In this section the focus is on developing communication skills that bring people together rather than drive them apart. Again, the issue of self-focus vs. reactivity is addressed. The emphasis is on becoming aware of how automatic negative reactive responses get you nowhere while consciously thought-out self-directed responses lead to progress.

There are two parts to communicating with another, listening and speaking. The concepts presented here are not complicated. However, they are difficult to achieve, because our reactivity gets in the way. To develop positive listening and speaking skills, one must work on overcoming negative self-talk and projection, focus on gaining a neutral, nonreactive perspective, and maintaining detachment while listening— definitely challenging when you are having a dispute with someone.

When psychotherapists are in training, the primary skills they seek to develop are effective listening and speaking. They are taught about empathy, which is defined as the ability to put yourself into another's experience in order to understand that person better. Everyone is capable of developing this skill, although some of us find it easier than others. Psychotherapists are also taught how to create an emotionally safe environment for the client, so that he or she will feel comfortable and safe enough to reveal problems. The therapist's task is not to tell the client what to do, but to create a safe setting and relationship that will allow the individual to get in touch with his or her own wisdom. This is not to say the therapist never gives advice. Sometimes he or she does, but the focus and goal of therapy is on the development of the self, to bring forth the client's own ability to problem solve, care for oneself, make decisions, and ultimately guide oneself through life using self-focus.

The essential ingredient in successful psychotherapy is the relationship between the therapist and the client, the therapeutic alliance. Unless the client feels accepted by the therapist exactly as he or she is, flaws and all, the relationship will not build and healing will not occur.

Relationships are about self and other. What makes the therapeutic relationship unique is that the therapist's task is to be there for the client without the expectation that the client will be there for the therapist. It is meant to be a one-way street. In the real world, relationships are not one-way streets. When we choose to be in a relationship, whether it be with a spouse, lover, relative, or friend, we expect to benefit from it and to experience give and take. Unfortunately, each of us has our own expectation of how the other should be there for us and, often, that other does not meet our expectations, so the relationship suffers.

Most of us are capable of taking the therapist's position with another, of being there for the other, at least for short periods of time. However, the process of being there for the other is most successful when it is experienced as a two-way street; that is, the individuals in the relationship take turns being there for each other. For various reasons, this is not always possible. For example, one person in the relationship may not be willing or may lack sufficient empathy to participate in the process. And in the case of interacting with children, the parent-child relationship *is* more of a one-way street. Regardless of whether your partner, lover, relative, or friend chooses to participate in the process of improving communication, learning the skills will benefit your relationships with others.

The next few coping skills address how problems are perpetuated by listening and speaking to others in ways that are harmful rather than helpful, and present techniques that therapists use to promote better communication between people.

12 • Try Not to Make the Other Person Wrong

Each of us lives our own life circumstances. Like snowflakes, no two are the same. We come to each moment in life with histories of experience and backgrounds that influence our reactions to events, the choices we make, and our points of view. When two people (or, for that matter, two countries) are in conflict, the greatest deterrent to reconciliation and peace is the tendency for each person to defend his or her own position rather than to work in an authentically heartfelt way to understand the other's side. When defensive positions are dropped, a shift occurs, because the attacks upon each other cease. Each person can be emotionally safe within the conflict, because no one is regarded as right or wrong. For the participants, the goal is not winning the argument but understanding the other's perspective. The conflict becomes a puzzle to be solved for the benefit of both, rather than a contest to be won.

Something basic that we all tend to assume, especially in our close relationships, is that people use their minds and experience life the same way. This perspective leads us to believe, "I can assume that since I think and experience things this way, other people do too, or at least they *should*." This assumption leads to miscommunications, because people don't experience events or think the same way.

Communicating with others without making them wrong is a way of living that fosters emotional health, psychological growth, and self-focus. Learning the skills to achieve this perspective is difficult, because it requires an interior shift from the ego's desire to win through judgment and blame to the higher purpose of conflict resolution through understanding.

One challenge that is difficult for most people to overcome in this process is achieving the detachment necessary to listen to the other's perspective without responding reactively with resentment, anger, and the need to defend and prove oneself right. For successful understanding and resolution to occur, the listener must feel an authentic desire to listen and take in the other's perspective. The listener must be able to set aside his or her feelings and agenda in the dispute, keep emotional reactions to what is being said at bay, accept the other's version as real and valid from his or her perspective, and try earnestly to understand without judgment.

13 • Listen Silently

When an individual listens to another's point of view in a heartfelt way with the authentic desire to understand, he or she focuses on the other completely and allows the other to talk without interruption. The listener strives to think about nothing except what the other is saying. This means the listener is not rehearsing comebacks to what is being said nor thinking about defensive responses. The listener's needs are not to be considered at this point in the communication process, only the speaker's. The listener sets aside his or her agenda in the dispute, for the moment, in order to focus on the other and take in the other's point of view.

The Way of Council (1996), by Jack Zimmerman and Virginia Cole, describes a process of communicating that is based on the wisdom circles of ancient and native people. Zimmerman and Cole adapted the wisdom circle dynamics to modern times for use in conflict resolution at schools, corporations, and in families. The process also works to resolve differences between two people.

Central to the council process is what is called the talking piece, which is held by the speaker. The person holding the talking piece is the only one who can speak. The talking piece empowers the holder to tell his or her story. In the case of conflict, it empowers the person to tell his or her side of the dispute. The story is told from a self-focused perspective, from the *I* position; "I'm going to tell you what my experience is in this situation, how it is for me. I'm not going to accuse you of anything. I'm not going to make you wrong. I'm just going to tell you the story of how I experience what is going on."

Storytelling does not require a response. Storytelling simply allows a person to get his or her story out. The listener's task is to truly hear and accept the storyteller's story without interrupting. A major problem in relationship conflict is that neither person gets the opportunity to express how they feel in an emotionally safe, nonjudgmental environment. While the speaker is holding the talking piece, the goal of the listener is to provide this setting for the speaker. Often, just getting feelings out brings great relief to the speaker, reducing anger, anxiety, and distress. Once one speaker has had a turn, he or she passes the talking piece to the other and then the speaker becomes the listener.

Remember Emily and John? One reason communication is so difficult for them is because neither is willing to consider the other's point of view. Each is invested in being right and proving the other wrong. Emily has said to John, "We need to find another way to communicate or I'm not going to talk about the children's behavior at all." John might respond to that by saying, "What other way? We're talking, aren't we? What other way is there?"

The problem here is that there are two parts to the communication process—speaking and listening. Most of us overlook the listening half, because we are preoccupied with winning the argument by convincing the other. This will not work, because it breeds alienation and hostility. To move forward, Emily and John need to listen to each other. They can begin the process of finding a new way to communicate by simply listening in a heartfelt way to the other's point of view.

14 • Passive Listening

Passive listening is another way of listening that lets the other person feel heard (Gordon 2000). Passive listening allows the speaker to talk about what is on his or her mind without being interrupted by judgmental comments, either positive or negative. Instead, the listener responds with brief and neutral comments that don't block the speaker's train of thought. The brief neutral comments encourage the speaker to keep talking because he or she feels accepted by the listener. In Dr. Thomas Gordon's book, *Parent Effectiveness Training*, these neutral comments are called "door openers," because they welcome the open expression of feelings about a problem.

Here is a dialogue from Gordon's book between a mother and her daughter. In this dialogue, the mother has set the goal for herself of providing a safe emotional setting for her daughter, so the daughter can openly process her feelings and have an opportunity to solve a problem on her own. From the self-focused *I* position, the mother will consciously work to keep her own reactive responses in check in order to avoid making judgmental comments about what her daughter reveals. The mother understands that being judgmental about what her daughter tells her will shut down the communication process, because the daughter will become defensive and resentful if her mother is critical. Therefore, the mother chooses to respond with door openers. As the dialogue unfolds, note how the child is able to gain insight and self-understanding. She reaches her own conclusions because her mother does not intrude by inserting positive or negative comments that interfere. The child is able to develop her own thinking and problem-solving abilities.

Child: I got sent down to the vice-principal's office today.

Parent: Oh?

Child: Yeah. Mr. Franks said I was talking too much in class.

Parent: I see.

Child: I can't stand that old guy. He sits up there and talks about his troubles or his grandchildren and expects us to be interested. It's so boring you'd never believe it.

Parent: Mm-hmm.

Child; You just can't sit in that class doing nothing! You'd go crazy. Jeannie and I sit there and make jokes when he's talking. Oh, he's just the worst teacher you can imagine. It makes me mad when I get a lousy teacher.

Parent: (Silence.)

Child: I do good with a good teacher, but if I get someone like Mr. Franks I just don't feel like learning anything. Why do they let that guy teach?

Parent: (Shrugs.)

Child: I suppose I should get used to it, 'cause I'm not always going to have good teachers. There are more lousy ones than good ones and if I let the lousy ones get me down, I'm not going to get the grades I need to get into a good college. I'm really hurting myself, I guess (p. 45).

Passive listening does not require a lot of thought or effort on the part of the listener. Therefore, it is fairly easy, although you do have to maintain detachment. Door openers are helpful to use with a resistant teenager or anyone else who seems reluctant to communicate. They are especially helpful when you don't really know how to deal with the person or situation at the time, but do not want to cut off communication. Using door openers can buy you time to think about what is going on before you decide what to do and—surprise, surprise!—the person may solve the problem just by talking it through with you. Other words and phrases that are door openers are: "Uh-huh. Really? No kidding. How about that? Interesting. Is that so? You did, huh? Tell me more. I'd like to hear about that" (Gordon 2000, 56).

There are many other words and phrases that are door openers. They are words and phrases that do not judge, either positively or negatively. Negative comments interfere with communication because they breed resentment and shut down communication. Positive comments interfere because the speaker may become invested in communicating what he or she thinks will bring approval from the listener rather than staying focused on what he or she is authentically thinking and feeling inside.

When someone has a problem, effective listening is nonjudgmental. This is often a difficult perspective to maintain, especially when that someone has a problem with you.

15 • Speak from the Self-Focused I Position

In a dispute, when the speaker accuses and blames the other, he or she usually uses the word *you*. For example:

Her perspective: You never help with the kids!

His perspective: You're always nagging at me!

Accusing and blaming statements are put-downs. They attack the other's self-esteem, make him or her defensive, and create hostility between the speaker and listener. When the speaker uses I-messages, he or she avoids the word *you*. An I-message is designed to communicate how the other's behavior impacts emotionally on the speaker. It is worded in a way that tries not to make the other person wrong. I-messages are worded like this:

Her perspective: I'm frustrated because I feel like I'm the only one taking care of the kids. They're out of control. I feel like giving up.

His perspective: I'm exhausted when I get home from work. The kids are loud and all over the place. I need to relax, so I go in the bedroom and shut the door.

By working on developing their speaking and listening skills, this couple can work toward resolving their problems.

16 • Avoid These Roadblocks

In *Parent Effectiveness Training* (2000), Thomas Gordon lists road-blocks that interfere with positive communication between parents and children (p. 49). I have adapted them here to show how we all communicate in ways that drive people away from us emotionally, rather than bring them closer. Here are some examples:

Judging: Results in anger, resentment, distancing, and damages the other's self-esteem:
>   "You just don't try."
>   "You're so mean!"
>   "It's your fault we're broke."
>   "You're impossible!"

Giving orders: Creates resentment, distance:
>   "Don't do that again."
>   "Leave me alone!"
>   "Stop being so negative."
>   "Don't talk to me like that!"

Threatening: Creates anger, resentment, disconnection, and distance:
>   "One more time and I'm leaving!"
>   "If you walk out that door now, you're not coming back."
>   "If nobody else is going to help, I quit."
>   "You don't try, so I won't either."

Advising: Blocks the other's ability to gain self-understanding when he or she has a problem to work through:

"If you made an effort to get along with Paul, you wouldn't be so irritated at work."

"Studying more each day would help to bring your grades up."

"You need to be more organized so you won't get so stressed about losing things."

"The other kids would like you more if you didn't boss them around so much."

Praising: Overlooks how the other is feeling and diverts the individual from the process of self-understanding and resolving the problem:

"You *are* very smart!"

"You *are* capable of doing that!"

"You *do* make good decisions."

"You *are* very handsome."

Ridiculing: Creates anger, resentment, hurt. Damages self-esteem. Damages relationship building. Results in relationship disconnection:

"You think you're so smart, but look what you've gotten yourself into now!"

"What a wimp!"

"That's the best you can do?"

"No wonder you can't get along with anybody!"

Questioning: Becomes what directs the problem-solving process rather than the speaker's train of thought:

"How are you feeling now about Jake?"

"Do you think you could give up smoking if you exercised more?"

"What else is bothering you about school?"

"If you quit your job, what would you do?"

Diverting: Minimizes feelings and overlooks the problem. Undercuts a problem-solving opportunity. Leaves the person feeling unheard and the problem considered unimportant:

"Let's just have a nice evening and talk about it later."

"Watch the football game and your mood will get better."

"You'll feel better in the morning."

"You are great at a lot of things. Forget about that."

Problems and issues get stuck inside us, and if we don't have the opportunity to talk them through with someone in a way that relieves the pressure, they fester, resulting in anxiety, depression, anger, and bitterness toward others and ourselves. The presence of a partner, friend, relative, or parent who will help us reach partial or full resolution around an issue by listening results in psychological growth and health, and contributes to relationship stability.

This is not to say that you never praise, give advice, or question another. These communication roadblocks apply specifically when someone presents you with a problem that he or she needs to solve. That person *owns* the problem. The goal is to create a safe emotional environment and become a sounding board so the individual has the opportunity to figure out the solution for him or herself.

17 • Listen and Respond Reflectively

Often when someone is upset, what that person *says* is the problem may not actually *be* the problem. The true problem is hidden, not yet realized. That is why being a nonjudgmental sounding board for someone is such an effective psychological tool. Your listening can allow the speaker to reach a deeper level of self-understanding.

For example, let us say that Emily is angry with John because he likes to go off hunting and fishing with his friends, leaving her behind with the children. She accuses him of being selfish and irresponsible. Actually, she may get upset when he leaves, because she has unresolved abandonment issues from childhood that she projects onto the situation. She may also have guilt issues, because she learned to please others to avoid being criticized, yelled at, or hit. She pleases her children instead of herself, because she feels guilty about leaving them, especially if they don't want her to go. She doesn't allow herself to have fun with friends, so she resents that John does.

Besides listening silently or with door openers, there is another way of listening and responding when someone is expressing a problem that can help the person get in touch with the underlying issue. It is a process of listening and responding reflectively; that is, reflecting back to the speaker, in your own words, what you think the person is trying to express. For instance, your son says to you, "I hate Brian. He's such a jerk." A reflective response would be, "It sounds like you're really upset with Brian." If you respond with "You shouldn't hate anybody," or "Don't call people names," you close off an opportunity to process what is going on with your child. Judgmental scolding shuts people down and ends meaningful communication.

Listening and responding reflectively is also effective with a spouse who has a problem or is angry with you. The safe emotional environment can allow the person to get in touch with the deeper issue through talking it out. The challenge for the listener is to reflect back accurately what the speaker is saying. This is not easy because one's natural inclination is to defend oneself if being personally attacked, or otherwise to help the speaker with the problem by offering encouragement, suggestions, or solutions. These approaches and others mentioned previously interfere with the speaker's ability to make progress around the issue (Gordon 2000).

The goal of the listener is to provide the circumstances that will allow the speaker to tune into what is going on inside emotionally to gain insight into why he or she is feeling upset. The job of the listener is to help the speaker clarify his or her point of view in order to gain self-understanding.

18 • Sample Dialogue:
Speaking from the Self-Focused I Position and
Listening and Responding Reflectively

When you are at odds with someone, the overall goal of participating in the process of speaking to the other from the self-focused *I* position, while the other listens and responds reflectively, is relationship improvement. The relationship improves because the process fosters understanding on two levels:

1. The speaker is allowed a safe, open emotional environment for expression, which can lead to a deeper level of self-understanding.
2. The listener gains understanding and insight by hearing the other's point of view.

What follow here are two dialogues between Emily and John. In the first, Emily is the speaker and John is the listener. In the second, the roles are reversed. The listener, who reflects back to the speaker what he or she thinks is being said, has a difficult role, because the listener must try to remain neutral and nonreactive no matter what is said. The speaker also has a difficult task—to speak from the self-focused *I* position without making the other person wrong.

At first, this way of communicating seems awkward, cumbersome, and even silly. The listener may have a hard time accurately rephrasing what the speaker says because the listener's own reactive responses get in the way. And the speaker may have difficulty expressing his or her position in the conflict without making the other person wrong. This technique works, though, and is worth the effort it takes to master it. Eventually, the awk-wardness of the language disappears and each person becomes more rela-tional, rather than competitive, in how he or she interacts with the other. With time, this way of communicating and relating can become automatic.

The issue John and Emily address in the dialogues is the boundary Emily has set with John about the way they communicate. She told him she will no longer discuss the children's behavior when he is angry, being mean, or verbally attacking her or the children. She said that unless they can find another way to communicate she will not discuss the children's behavior at all. John finally agrees to try communicating in a different way.

Dialogue I

Here Emily speaks from the self-focused *I* position, and John listens and responds reflectively:

Emily: I get so upset when I hear the children being yelled at or I'm being yelled at or criticized!

John: You get very upset when you hear criticism and yelling.

Emily: I can't stand it! It makes me feel sick. I can't even think!

John: It makes you feel sick and you can't even think.

Emily: I wish it didn't bother me so much, but it does and I can't control it.

John: You wish yelling and criticism didn't bother you so much, but you can't control it.

Emily: Yes and I can't live with the children being treated this way. It has to change.

John: You can't live with it and it has to change.

Emily: I know the kids make things worse. They are out of control, but I don't know what to do about it.

John: You know the kids are out of control and make things worse, but you don't know what to do about it.

Emily: I do know that the yelling makes me feel like I did when I was a kid. Nothing I ever did was right then. And it's the same way now. I just can't please anybody. I feel like I'm going crazy.

John: When you were a kid you felt like you do now—yelled at and criticized and you feel like you're going crazy.

Emily: Yes.

Note: At the end of this dialogue, Emily has gained insight into why she becomes so emotionally charged when she is being yelled at or criticized.

Dialogue II

Here John speaks from the self-focused *I* position, and Emily listens and responds reflectively:

John: Well, I hate the way your kids treat us, especially the way they treat you. It enrages me!

Emily: You hate how the kids treat us, especially me. It makes you very angry.

John: You do everything for them and they do nothing in return. They make messes and expect you to clean them up. You clean up the kitchen, then turn around and they've messed it up again. It's unbelievable!

Emily: It's unbelievable how the kids do nothing to help, but make messes and expect me to clean up.

John: You said it! Those kids are learning nothing about responsibility. I get so mad when I see them walk all over you. I just want to shake you, make you see it.

Emily: You want to shake me, make me see that the kids are learning nothing about responsibility.

John: I love you, but it's getting harder and harder to stay here. I'm irritated and angry all the time. You don't listen to a thing I say. My feelings and opinions don't count. It's your house, your furniture, your kids. I have no say at all.

Emily: It's hard for you to stay here because you're so mad all the time. Everything is mine, and what you say doesn't count.

John: Yes.

Note: Here John is able to communicate that he feels powerless in the family dynamic. At this point in the dialogue, their two issues have been expressed: Emily's reaction to criticism and yelling and John's feeling of being powerless. The dialogue can end or continue now, depending on whether either person has something more to say. If the dialogue ends, it is best to stop any discussion about the subject and have each person go his or her own way, allowing time for each to absorb what was said without reacting.

The preceding dialogues are made up. They are designed to depict common problems that exist in relationships, especially families, and to provide examples of how to speak from a self-focused *I* perspective and how to respond reflectively. In the real world, when two people are upset, especially when first learning this communication technique, the dialogues probably will not go as well as depicted here. It is the norm for both self-focus and control of reactivity to be lost at times during the dialogue. Successfully learning to communicate this way requires patience and practice. What is important is that each person be willing to try to develop the skills, and to be tolerant and forgiving of the other if emotional control is lost.

Having said this, there is another point to be made: Sometimes one person in the conflict is not willing or is unable (because of a lack of empathic ability) to participate in the listening and reflective process. This means that you listen to the other, but the other does not take a turn listening to your side. This is frustrating for the listener and seems unfair. However, progress can be made by just one person reflecting what the other says, because the other feels heard, and this alone can relieve tension and change the dynamics of the relationship. If your goal is to improve the relationship, then *you* just listening and reflecting what the other says can be worth the effort.

Also, there are times when taking turns listening to each other is not needed. For instance, if your child comes home from school upset about something that happened that day, listening and responding reflectively can help the child work through the problem. Or if a friend is having marital problems, reflecting what he or she says can clarify issues and lead to possible solutions for your friend. In these cases the listening is a one-way street.

19 • Conflict Resolution: Find Solutions that Work for All

A simple method for conflict resolution is to find a solution, or solutions, that work for all (Gordon 2000).

Let's return to Emily and John: John says he hates how the children treat Emily and him, and he feels that he has no say about what happens in the family. He gets mad, yells, and criticizes. Emily cannot tolerate the yelling and criticism and has set a boundary with John that she will not talk about the children's behavior when John is angry, yelling, and criticizing. The conflict resolution process calls for each person to brainstorm proposed solutions to the problem and, together, make a list of the proposed solutions. Here's an example:

John: The children should spend more time with their father so Emily and I can have more alone time.

Emily: John should stop telling the children what to do.

John: Emily should take a parenting class to learn to parent the children better.

Emily: John and I should go to couples' counseling.

John: The children should have regular chores and have consequences if they don't do them.

Emily: I will be the disciplinarian of the children, not John.

John: I will have more input into family and household decisions.

Emily: John will not yell or criticize.

John: If I don't yell and criticize, Emily needs to put in a genuine effort to understand, accept, and consider my point of view.

Emily: John needs to work on being more tolerant of how I handle things, especially when I'm trying to make the changes he wants.

After the brainstorming process, each person has the opportunity to cross out a solution that is unacceptable to him or her, no questions asked. There needs to be complete freedom around this process. One does not judge the other's rejection of a proposed solution. The conflict resolution process will not work unless the final solutions are genuinely embraced by both parties (Gordon 2000). If all the proposed solutions become crossed out, then the brainstorming process begins anew. Once the crossing-out process is complete and Emily and John accept the remaining solutions, they can begin trying to make them work. If they come upon more difficulties as they try to make the solutions work, they can repeat the process to uncover more solutions. Acceptance of each other's viewpoints, the ability to detach and not make the other person wrong, and maintaining self-focus are the key skills to develop while working through this process.

III

Couples

III

Copias

20 • Couples Beware! Many Pitfalls Await You.

When individuals fall in love and choose to share their lives, they assume they will be able to manage the problems and conflicts that will come their way. In reality, though, they can be like insects flying into spider webs, because hidden psychological traps may await them. Without awareness of the traps, the couple can become so entangled in them that the relationship is doomed. All these traps are created by their lack of awareness of unseen, unconscious past-related dramas being played out between them. By becoming conscious of the hidden dramas and the traps, they can gain insight and dismantle them.

Some of the psychological traps that ensnare couples have already been discussed:

1. One person (or both) does not have a strong self-identity or self-focus and lacks the ability to self-care. He or she tries to please the other in order to make the relationship "work." The individual cannot say "no," set boundaries, or create self-directed goals. This lack of a sense of self-worth eventually leads to symptoms of anxiety or depression. The person becomes angry and bitter toward the other, but does not express the feelings.

2. One's past negative or traumatic experiences are projected onto present circumstances or the other person. This can cause one to overreact, become highly emotional, and read into what someone is saying, or into a situation, something that is not actually there. Projection produces a highly charged emotional response that is destructive to both the relationship and the individual reacting.

3. One person (or both) cannot detach emotionally from what is going on or being said. He or she takes things too personally. Detaching gives one the ability to gain a neutral perspective, to think more rationally, and to respond to another from a more controlled self-directed perspective.

4. When disagreeing, each person tends to want to win the argument rather than understand the other's point of view. The back and forth dispute creates distance between the couple instead of bringing them together. This interferes with conflict resolution.

Other traps that catch couples are unsafe emotional environments, pursuer-distancer dynamics, conflicts that result because men generally have a competitive nature and women a more relational one, and mate-guarding. Also, people have different personality types that influence how they think and the choices they make. Certain couple combinations of these types produce stress. The different personality types will be addressed in Section VI.

21 • Assess Your Relationship for Its Emotional Environment

The kind of emotional environment that develops as a couple is together determines whether the individuals feel emotionally safe and relatively content or emotionally unsafe, anxious, and unhappy. Overall, the more people are free to be themselves without fear of blame, the more pleasant the environment and the greater chance that both partners' esteem will thrive.

In an atmosphere of tolerance and acceptance, thoughts and ideas are freely exchanged, and people feel mutually supported and safely connected. In an atmosphere that is intolerant, overly controlled, or where there is negative judgment, criticism, and competition for who is right, thoughts and ideas are guarded, and people do not feel mutually supported or safely connected.

Each person in a couple comes into the relationship as a unique individual. The most successful couples are those who can balance the sense of togetherness needed to feel like a couple with the sense of separateness required to maintain a strong self-identity. One's sense of self is formed in childhood and maintained in adulthood through the quality of one's relationships and achievements. An adult who comes from a critical or abusive environment will have more difficulty achieving and maintaining a strong sense of self as part of a couple than one who comes from an accepting family background. And someone who comes from an abusive background is more likely to perpetuate or suffer abusive treatment than someone who has not.

Is the emotional atmosphere that surrounds your relationship safe, friendly, and supportive? Do you feel free to be yourself? Or do you walk on eggshells around your partner because he or she is controlling, critical, easily angered? Are you anxious and afraid to be yourself?

22 • Maintaining Self-Identity in the Couple Relationship

The word *ego* is Latin and translates into English as *I*. The ego is the psychological structure that enables us to be aware and experience ourselves in a way that other mammals and primates cannot. This psychological structure is what provides the sense of self. No matter how old I am or whether I'm thin or fat, throughout my lifetime, I will experience myself as myself.

The ego personality is what animates the body uniquely and makes each person distinct. It is the life force and is ever seeking to realize its potential. If the emotional atmosphere that surrounds a couple is so critical and combative that the personality is squelched in one or both individuals, strife and unhappiness will result.

For an example, let us return to Emily and John:

As mentioned before, John likes to go hunting and fishing with his friends. Hunting and fishing are age-old male activities that can reinforce his sense of himself as a man. He enjoys camaraderie with his buddies by being with them while hunting and fishing. He may also enjoy just being in the woods, on a lake, river, or at sea—away from stress. He may find peace there. He is happier, therefore, when he has the chance to go hunting and fishing.

Emily feels abandoned when he goes. Because she does, she makes him miserable before he leaves and harps at him about how selfish he is when he returns. As a result, he cannot completely enjoy the trip and may even question the rightness of his going. While away he may feel guilty and dread going back home because of what he will face when he gets there. In a sense, then, he is not completely on the trip. Part of his mind is with Emily, and worrying. In this way, he becomes divided within himself, fractured; that is, he is not completely with himself while away.

On the other hand, if John were with someone who did not have abandonment issues but instead a strong sense of self, she might encourage him to go on the trip by saying, "Sure, honey. Go. I'm glad you have the chance to get away and have some fun." Under these circumstances John *could* be completely present and with himself on the trip—no guilt, no anxiety about what he will face when he gets home. Instead he will fully experience the pleasure of the trip and the rejuvenation of spirit it can provide.

The situation would have been even worse for John, though, if he had given into Emily's pressure and not gone at all. Then, not only would he have lost the benefits the trip could provide, but he would also feel angry and bitter toward Emily because she kept him from going. The more he gives into her under these circumstances, the unhappier he will become.

In order for these dynamics to change, John needs to get in touch with how he is feeling and figure out what he wants to do about it. He needs to gain self-focus, detach, set a boundary with Emily, and follow through.

23 • Be Aware of Purser/Distancer Dynamics

In most relationships, there is an emotional pursuer and an emotional distancer. In Emily and John's case, Emily is the pursuer and John is the distancer. In a safe emotional setting, these differences have the effect of keeping the individuals balanced between being separate as individuals and together as a couple (Guerin et al 1987).

People have different styles of relating to each other emotionally. Some are more open to emotional expression and intimacy than others. These differences occur naturally because of personality differences and the different ways men and women generally prefer to relate to each other.

Emotionally, most women are relationship based; that is, they feel most secure when they feel emotionally connected to the people they love. Most men are competition based emotionally. They love their families but feel most secure when they feel in control of a situation and can handle it. They can become uncomfortable with emotional displays and the insistence from their partner for emotional closeness. Something confusing for a woman is that just as she feels closest to her partner, he pulls away. For many men, being close emotionally makes them feel weak, vulnerable, and unsafe. They pull away to rebalance themselves— to feel competent, strong, and in control again.

In an unsafe emotional environment or under stress, pursuer/distancer dynamics intensify conflict. The two styles of relating develop because the individuals have different ways of maintaining their inner balance and emotional calm—one by feeling emotionally connected, the other by feeling emotionally independent. When the couple is stressed:

1. Both spouses react by moving in the direction of restoring their own levels of internal emotional comfort, becoming more like themselves: the wife as pursuer moves toward her husband, the distancer, for emotional connection in an attempt to restore inner calm, while the husband moves away toward objects and activity, also in an effort to restore inner calm.

2. At the very moment when the pursuer needs connectedness more than ever, her partner is distancing even more than usual. Just when the distancer needs to be left alone to calm down, he sees his wife coming at him spilling prodigious amounts of emotion. This pattern creates additional anxiety for both spouses, raises their level of emotional arousal, and intensifies still further their emotional reactivity to one another. The cycle of pursuit and distance intensifies even more (Guerin et al 1987, 47).

This cycle can occur over and over, keeping the two in an ongoing state of reactivity. The pursuer cannot get the sense of emotional safety needed through connection, and the distancer cannot get the space needed to calm down and feel in control.

The way to break the cycle is for the pursuer to stop pursuing. For the pursuer to stop, he or she needs to get reactive responses under control, gain self-focus, detach, stop taking the distancer's behavior as a personal affront, and give the distancer the space he or she needs. Then the distancer can find the emotional conditions needed to rebalance and come back to the relationship. The equilibrium of the couple can be reestablished (Ibid.).

24 • Watch out for Mate-Guarding and Female Submission

Here's some bad news. We each have an unconscious primate nature that can arise and cause trouble, especially between men and women. In nonhuman primates, like chimpanzees, orangutans and gorillas, males are driven by the mating effort and females by the parenting effort. We are too.

The nonhuman primate male strategy for ensuring the survival of the fittest is to gain dominance. Males fight for breeding rights. The strong overcome the weak. When the dominant male has established his supremacy, then he must guard and fight off any advances toward his females from other males. This is called mate-guarding and guarantees his reproductive success.

On the other hand, the nonhuman female primates learn another strategy for survival. Because they are surrounded by violent males, they learn to read facial expressions and body language to assess for danger to avoid it. They learn to provide sexual favors to strong males to gain protection for themselves and their young. They learn to be submissive when that is the only choice for survival (Geary 1998).

Both men and women mate-guard today, but men are more prone to it. When a relationship is characterized by one partner dominating another in a mate-guarding fashion, it can lead to domestic violence. If you are in a new relationship and see evidence of mate-guarding—that is, unreasonable jealousy and over controlling behavior—run. If you are in a long-term relationship where mate-guarding is a problem, get help from a counselor or get out as safely as you can by contacting the domestic violence services in your community.

IV

The Family

25 • Assess Your Family for Its Underlying Structural Dynamics

Once a child is born, a couple becomes a family, and the psychological interplay that goes on among individuals gets more complicated. How the individuals will interact throughout family life together will depend on how well each can develop and maintain self-focus and positive self-regard. The parents are the ones who set the stage for how family life unfolds. How they set this stage is also dependent upon how they were treated as children.

Murray Bowen and Salvador Minuchin are two family therapists who developed ways of treating family problems by working to change the underlying structure, or system, that determines how family members interact, rather than dealing with specific issues that cause conflict between family members. Salvadore Minuchin's perspective:

> Family structure [is] the organized pattern in which families interact... it describes sequences that are predictable...As family transactions are repeated, they foster expectations that establish enduring patterns. Once patterns are established, family members use only a small fraction of the range of behaviors available to them. The first time the baby cries, or the in-laws come to visit, or a teenager misses the school bus, it's not clear who will do what. Will the load be shared? Will there be a quarrel? Soon, however, patterns are set, roles assigned, and things take on a sameness and predictability. "Who's going to...?" becomes "She'll probably..." and then "She always...." (Nichols and Schwartz 1998, 244).

"Structural family therapy is a blueprint for analyzing the process of family interactions. Without a map you're lost—caught up in the detailed content of family discussions with no overall plan" (Ibid.).

Central to the approach of structural family therapy are the concepts of first-order change and second-order change. First-order change addresses problems superficially. Although one particular issue may be resolved, the way the family functions remains the same. Family patterns that determine acceptable or unacceptable behavior do not change, and the patterns are what perpetuate the disharmony. Second-order change goes deeper. It identifies family patterns. Those that don't work are discarded. Family members gain insight and come up with new ways of interacting (Nichols and Schwartz 1998).

For instance, back to Emily and John: If Emily had chosen to set a boundary with her children to address disrespectful behavior (instead of with John about the communication issue), she might have said to them, "You are grounded until your attitudes improve and you start doing your chores." If the children had complied to avoid punishment, this would be an example of first-order change only because, although particular issues would have been singled out, the underlying relationship and communication dysfunction would not have been addressed. As a result, family members would continue battling. Second-order change is achieved when the underlying issues are brought to light, sorted through, and rectified. The goal in structural family therapy is to bring about second-order change.

26 • Terms Used in Structural Family Therapy

Understanding how structural family therapy terms relate to family dynamics can help sort out what is going on in a family.

Dyad means a pair. A couple is a dyad. Although the psychological dynamics that occur in a couple relationship can be complicated and confusing, they are not as complex as those that develop in a family. The more family members there are, the more complex things get. The parental dyad sets the stage for how family life plays out. Key influences for the successful functioning of the parental dyad are:

1. The parents' conscious awareness of family dynamics. Are they tuned into what is going on?
2. The capacity that each individual in the pair has for self-focus.
3. The capacity the parents have for good communication with each other.
4. Their joint determination to create a safe emotional environment for each member of the family.
5. Their ability to provide effective containment around their children's behavior when it is harmful to self and others.

This is such a huge and difficult job that nobody gets it right all the time. However, awareness of typical underlying structural dynamics that lead to trouble can go a long way toward avoiding problems.

A **triangle** is created as soon as a baby is born to a couple. This triangle can become a problem immediately, because the mother is usually the primary caregiver. During the first year, she and the baby may bond closer than father and baby, so the father feels left out. Mother and baby become a dyad. If the father is the primary caregiver, father and baby become a dyad and the mother feels left out. This alignment of mother and child or father and child can continue when other children are born. Mother and children or father and children can become a group that interacts in exclusive ways that leave out the other parent.

The existence of triangles can be very destructive to family members and family life. Remember how you felt in high school when you felt excluded? Family members who are excluded from intimate family groupings suffer. Many kinds of triangles form. If there are two or more children, one child may feel excluded. Stepfamily triangles are particularly difficult, especially when children feel cut off emotionally from a parent when the parent takes on a new partner. The children can feel excluded from a former close parental relationship and resent the new partner because of it. On the other hand, the new partner may feel excluded because the parent and children have a long history together and established ways of connecting and interacting. Extended family triangles also form. For instance, a woman and her mother may align against the woman's spouse. Adult sisters can align against another sister or brother. Whenever one person talks to another about a third, or when one person feels pulled emotionally between the wants and needs of two others, a triangle is formed.

A **cross-generational coalition** is an alliance between a parent and a child against another family member, often the other parent. These coalitions indicate that the structure of the family is off. For the family to be in balance, the parents need to be aligned as a dyad and in charge. Cross-generational coalitions form because, for one reason or another, the parents become estranged and emotionally distant from each other. In order to gain emotional support from somewhere, one parent (or sometimes both) attaches to one or another of the children in an inappropriate emotional way, sharing problems and seeking comfort. The inappropriate alliance can cause ongoing problems, as shown in the following example, which depicts both a cross-generational coalition and a triangle:

A mom has a relationship with her teenage son where she talks to him about issues she has with his father. She also talks to him about some of her problems at work. Because she does not get emotional support from her husband, she seeks it from her son.

One Sunday, Dad gives his son the chore of cleaning out the garage. Son puts off doing the job all week. Finally on Friday night Dad says, "Unless the garage is cleaned out by tomorrow night, you're not going out!"

Son objects because he has plans with friends Saturday morning and a football game in the afternoon. Saturday night comes around, the garage is not done, and Dad says, "You're not going out!"

Son gets upset and talks to his mother. "Mom, I've finally gotten a date with Haley tonight and Dad won't let me go. This'll ruin everything. I have to go."

Mom says, "But you didn't clean out the garage."

Son says, "I know, but I will tomorrow. I promise.

Mom says, "Well, I know this date means a lot to you. You absolutely promise to do it tomorrow."

Son says, "Absolutely, Mom, absolutely.

Mom talks to Dad. Dad gives in. The next day, the garage may or may not get cleaned out.

This kind of dynamic leads to endless quarrels in a family because the family alignment is out of kilter. The person in charge here is the son. Mom and Dad need to work on developing their communication skills. They need to decide together how they want to handle the garage chore before talking to their son. Once they can operate as a team (easier said than done), they can change their family structure to bring about second-order change.

Subsystems are sets of relationships within a family, like cliques. For example, two teenagers in a family may have more open communication and fun together than they do with another sibling. Two other typical subsystems have already been mentioned—Mom and children connect better than they do with Dad or vice-versa, or the biological parent and children are emotionally bonded in a way that excludes a step-parent.

Interpersonal boundaries are invisible walls between people that regulate emotional and physical closeness and distance. Here are three examples:

Diffuse boundaries are not clearly defined, are too open, and easily broken through. Parents and children are overly involved with each other in inappropriate ways. The parents' leadership role is undermined by arguments with each other and with the children. The family bickers and fights.

Rigid boundaries create such strong divisions among family members that emotional support and connections are cut off. One or both parents may be highly critical and unapproachable. A typical family dynamic is that one parent, usually the mother, is overly involved with the children because of diffuse boundaries, and the father is under-involved because of boundaries that are too rigid (Nichols and Schwartz 1998).

Clear boundaries appropriately define family relationships and the hierarchical structure of the family as top down from parents to children. The parents are the leaders, but approachable and open to family discussions about problems.

From the structural family therapy perspective, "What distinguishes a normal family isn't the absence of problems, but a functional family structure" (Nichols and Schwartz 1998, 245). The subsystems are in the functional positions of parents as one subsystem, siblings as another. The roles of parents and children are defined by clear boundaries rather than boundaries that are rigid or diffuse.

27 • Murray Bowen's Perspective

Murray Bowen's family systems theory examines concepts that he labels as differentiation of self, interlocking triangles, the family projection process, and the multigenerational transmission process. Although his family therapy theory identifies the family as a system, rather than a structure, when assessing your own family, it can be helpful to envision his concepts structurally as well. His perspective determines whether family members are differentiated (self-focused and independent) or undifferentiated (too emotionally involved and reactive). His point of view sorts out family triangles and determines how they are harmful. He examines the unresolved issues between parents that they project onto the children and determines how patterns of dysfunction are passed on from one generation to another.

Differentiation of self: According to Bowen, the major problem in families is emotional fusion; the major goal is differentiation.

> Emotional fusion grows out of an instinctual need for others, but is an unhealthy exaggeration of this need. Some people manifest fusion directly as a need for togetherness; others mask it with a pseudo-independent façade. The person with a differentiated self need not be isolated, but can stay in contact with others and maintain his or her integrity (Nichols and Schwartz, 172).

For Bowen, differentiation is achieved through the capacity one has to separate feeling from thinking. His view is that, without this capacity, the individual cannot be objective about a family situation because his or her intellect is too flooded by emotions. Undifferentiated family members are so caught up reactively that they can't gain a separate perspective or sense of themselves as emotionally independent. Differentiated individuals can separate their rational selves from their emotional selves, gain perspective, and become independent.

Interlocking triangles: Bowen regards family problems as rooted in triangles. To determine a family's structure, he examines how family members are triangulated within the primary family unit, and within the extended families of both parents. "…how interlocking triangles connect one generation to the next—like threads interwoven in a total family fabric…." (Nichols and Schwartz 1998, 172).

The family projection process: Tension and conflict between parents leads to emotional distance and then to conflict avoidance. The parents distance from each other to avoid the discomfort of addressing their own problems. They create a triangle that puts the children's issues, usually those of one child, between them so they can focus away from their own tensions. The child, rather than the issues between the parents, becomes the problem. This child is the symptom bearer of the family's dysfunction and the most reactive to the family's emotional circumstances.

> The child who is the object of the projection becomes the most attached to the parents (positively or negatively) and the one with the least differentiation of self…the child eventually develops symptoms of psychological impairment, necessitating further parental concern and solidifying the family pattern (Ibid.).

Once the structure of the family is altered to bring about second-order change, the child is released from the reactive position.

The multi-generational transmission process: Bowen's perspective is that family interactions are set within the multigenerational family system; that is, passed down from one generation to the next. Because the problems in the family system are related to unresolved problems between the parents, and their problems are related to the problems between each of their sets of parents, a generational approach is needed.

If you want to figure out your family's structure, examine these questions: Are you and your partner a dyad? Do triangles exist and do they also exist in relation to extended family members? Do cross-generational coalitions exist? That is, are either you or your spouse emotionally aligned with one of the children in an inappropriate way? Assess the subsystems. Are they appropriately arranged with top-down leadership from parents to children? What kind of boundaries are there in your family? Are they diffuse (too easily broken through), which result in lots of arguments? Are they rigid, cutting people off from each other emotionally? Or are they clear so that everyone knows where they stand while at the same time staying safely emotionally connected?

Are family members differentiated or not? Do they function from a self-focused perspective, or are they overly emotional and highly reactive to one another? Are there unresolved issues between you and your partner that you avoid confronting by diverting attention onto the children's problems or those of one child through the family projection process? Is there a child in your family who is carrying the burden of the family's problems and acting out, overly anxious, or depressed? And what are the unresolved issues that have been handed down to your family from your family of origin and that of your spouse by way of the multi-generational transmission process?

By becoming aware of unresolved problems and working to solve them, you can pave the way for you and your partner to move from responding to each other reactively to each gaining self-focus. By changing the relationship between the two of you and becoming conscious of other structural family issues, you can alter the structure of your family and bring about second-order change.

V

Parenting

28 • Understand How the Will of the Ego-Self Develops in a Child

In a child, the will of the ego-self relentlessly pushes to assert itself because it is ever striving to *become*. Its drive and goal orientation is based upon the genetically programmed need we all have to become independent and established in the world on our own. The ego's drive is the natural force within each of us that steers us to overcome dependence. Unfortunately it results in situations where the three-year-old refuses to put on pajamas, brush teeth, or go to bed. The refrains heard by parents at this age are, "No!" or "I do it. Me can do it." This drive to become independent is particularly hard to deal with in teenagers who think they are invincible, know it all, and may refuse to cooperate about anything and everything. So, in addition to needing nurturance and a safe supportive emotional environment, children need containment and guidance around what they can be allowed to do and how they behave. This sets up a friction between parents and children that is ongoing. Problems occur because children want more independence than they are capable of managing, so power struggles arise between parents and children. This dynamic is what makes the job of parenting so difficult.

Our society depends on *power over* to control children, but the power over way of parenting works against the drive of the ego-self, which seeks to realize itself and become independent. Besides, a relationship that relies on power over never works, because the self of the one who is not in the power position is not allowed expression, and this creates resentment. In an overly controlled environment, the child reacts in one of two ways as he or she gets older, either by becoming overly compliant, the self damped down, or, more often, angry and rebellious. In both cases, self-development is hampered.

The power over way of parenting sets up a competition between parent and child about who is right and who is wrong. Over and over, as the child is judged negatively and made to feel wrong, he or she becomes bitter, hostile, and distanced, and battles escalate. The competitive right-wrong dynamic intensifies as the child gets older. Finally, as parent and child stand eye to eye, the power over approach just does not work and parental control is lost. A more consciously thought-out way to parent is to foster a relational approach that encourages self develoment (as presented in Section II) rather than damps it down. Granted, there are times when parents have to resort to power over to be in control of what a child does or does not do, but the less often this happens, the better.

Contending with the drive of a child's will in ways that damage self-esteem, rather than building it, is where parents go wrong. The parents' job is to encourage age-appropriate independence while at the same time providing guidance in areas where the child is too inexperienced to make decisions. It is like a dance—a very difficult one—between providing freedom and containment.

29 • Gain Self Psychology Awareness

A baby is always born into a situation that is not of his or her own making. Today, almost a third of the children born in the United States are born into nontraditional family settings. The parents are not together. The family structure is not clearly defined, and the future wellbeing of these children is less certain because of the lack of two-parent support. Despite this, children born into any situation can thrive if they experience one common circumstance—a supportive environment that ensures appropriate nurturance and emotional and physical safety. Under these conditions, the self of a child can evolve into a strong, cohesive internal structure with the capacity to develop a differentiated and self-focused perspective in adulthood. Children born into circumstances where nurturance is not available and they are not emotionally and physically safe develop self-structures in adulthood that are not differentiated. They are wounded, fragile, fractured, and destined to try to defend themselves reactively in ways that are destructive to the individual and society:

> The most fundamental finding of self psychology is that the emergence of the self requires more than the inborn tendency to organize experience. Also required is the presence of others, technically designated as *objects* who provide certain types of experiences that will evoke the emergence and maintenance of the self. The perhaps awkward term for these is selfobject experiences. Proper selfobject experiences favor the structural cohesion and energetic vigor of the self; faulty selfobject experiences facilitate the fragmentation of the self. Along with food and oxygen, every human being requires age-appropriate selfobject experiences from infancy to the end of life… (Wolfe 1988, 11).

Heinz Kohut, a neurologist who fled the Nazi occupation of Vienna, Austria in 1939, settled in Chicago, and developed the school of psychological thought known as self psychology. The view of self psychology is that the self-structure in a human being is formed through an individual's interactions with the outer world—people, objects, circumstances, situations, and events—what Kohut calls selfobject experiences. The most important selfobject experiences in a child's life are with people— between self and other—especially with caregivers. Since the inner structure of the self is created through interactions with the outer world, the parents' influence on that self-creation is primary.

A child in relation to his or her caregivers is like a person standing in front of a mirror. The caregivers are the mirror that reflects the self-image into the child as each interaction occurs, moment-to-moment. If a child is called stupid and made to feel like he or she is bad or incapable, that is the self image that is created within. On the other hand, if the child is praised, encouraged, and feels safe emotionally, the positive reflection by caregivers creates a positive self supporting structure within. As a mature adult, the inner voice of the individual will be self-directed, self-affirming, and confident. So the goal of effective parenting is to provide mirroring experiences for your child that will result in an independent, strong, cohesive self structure when your child becomes an adult.

> If a person is to feel well—to feel good about himself, with a secure sense of self, enjoying good self-esteem and functioning smoothly and harmoniously without undue anxiety and depression—he must experience himself consciously or unconsciously as surrounded by the responsiveness of others. The mode of this responsiveness varies from simple to complex and changes age appropriately (Wolfe 1988, 39).

Children who are harshly treated and negatively mirrored by caregivers develop fragmented disorganized self structures. They usually become either timid and fearful or angry and aggressive as adults—or worse—schizophrenic, paranoid, psychotic, psychopathic, suicidal, or homicidal. Self psychology regards such mental states as self disorders, the result of faulty selfobject experiences (Wolfe 1988).

Someone with a cohesive self-structure, either child or adult, is more tolerant of others and better able to work through the difficulties, disappointments, and frustrations we all face in the ups and downs of life. Someone with a fractured self-structure has less tolerance of others and, depending on the severity of the self-fractured state, little ability to control emotional reactions to frustrations, especially when an attack on self-esteem is experienced. If the self-state is very fragile to begin with, any threat triggers a highly reactive emotionally charged self-defending state. Individuals with relatively cohesive self-structures can generally tolerate self-esteem attacks and rebalance themselves. Those with severely self-fractured states cannot. These self-defending reactive states are called *regressions* in self psychology. They can result in dire consequences. "Frantic lifestyles, drug abuse, perversions, and delinquency all serve as desperate measures to hold on to some self organization and avoid sliding into the fragmented state" (Ibid., 43).

School bullies are examples of children who pick on others to gain equilibrium around their own self-fractured states. The children they pick on are usually vulnerable ones with little self-structure themselves. The bullying fractures the bullied more, and so irrationally, out of desperation and the need to gain self equilibrium, sometimes the bullied arm themselves, go to school, and shoot people.

> The person who *regresses* from a state of cohesion to one of partial or total loss of structure experiences this as a loss of self-esteem, or as a feeling of emptiness or depression or worthlessness or anxiety…fragmentation is sometimes experienced as the terrifying certainty of imminent death, which signals a process of apparently irreversible dissolution of the self. The experience of a crumbling self is so unpleasant that people will do almost anything to escape the perceptions brought about by fragmentation (Wolfe 1988, 39).

The bullied child, usually one who does not fit in and has an abusive background of self-fracturing experiences as well, becomes the school shooter because he is taken to such a painful state of self dissolution by the harassment of others that his reaction is to kill to preserve what is left of the crumbled self state. He makes this choice even though he may only experience this rebalancing for the few seconds it takes him, after the mayhem, to raise the gun and shoot himself.

Fortunately, the perspective of self psychology is that caregivers are human, flawed, and do not parent well all the time. Sometimes they are tired, impatient, out of sorts, or just fed up, and tempers are lost. So the self psychology philosophy recognizes that parents are not perfect and also recognizes that to be successful as parents, they do not need to be perfect. However, for the healthy self-structure to form in a child, self psychologists teach that parental interactions with children, day-to-day, over the span of childhood, *do* need to be *good enough*.

Consciously thought-out good-enough parenting gives your child the opportunity to develop into who he or she is meant to be by nature— to reach adulthood with self-confidence, self-focus, and the chance to live guided authentically from within. Consciously thought-out good-enough parenting cannot happen, though, unless you get control of your own reactive responses and gain the ability to parent from a self-focused perspective. Many of the strategies presented in previous sections support parenting skills that can build a healthy self-structure in your child. Here is a review of the skills as they apply to parenting.

Live in the Moment: Responding effectively to events that happen in the moment with your child is the focus here. Your son's or daughter's childhood unfolds moment by moment until it is over when he or she becomes a young adult. How you handle things moment-to-moment is what makes all the difference.

In Section I, *Live in the Moment* is presented as a coping skill for dealing with thoughts about the past or future that go round and round, getting you nowhere except upset. Focusing on what you are doing in the moment becomes the way to distract yourself from thoughts caught in the past or future that bring on depression or anxiety. When dealing with children, however, problems usually *do* occur in the moment and require some kind of response. This review of the coping skills is designed to help you maintain self-focus moment-to-moment when interacting with your child to minimize harmful reactive responses.

Gain a Self-Focused vs. Reactive Perspective*:* Gaining self-focus, rather than being emotionally reactive around how you parent, can make the difference between providing selfobject experiences that build the self-structure in your child as opposed to those that fracture it. Maintaining self-focus is a discipline—not of your children, but of yourself. When a problem occurs in the moment with a child or children, we are accustomed to responding immediately and usually reactively. In most instances, though, something that can bring forth a much better outcome is to *not* react or respond immediately; rather, give yourself time to think things through from a self-focused perspective.

Don't Say "Yes" When You Want to Say "No": If a yes or no response is needed, give yourself time to think about how you *want* to respond from a self-focused perspective, rather than responding automatically and reactively. Some parents say "yes" because they feel guilty saying "no." If you mostly please your children, rather than yourself, eventually you will resent them, and your relationship with them will suffer because of it. On the other hand, some parents automatically say "no;" then children become distant, resentful, and angry.

Quiet the Negative, Fearful, Worrying Voice: Almost always, day-to-day, it is our reactions to disturbing events that happen, rather than the events themselves, that escalate upset. By finding ways to talk to yourself that support your parenting effort and calm you down rather than make you more upset, you will handle a situation better. Usually you do not have to respond immediately to something that has happened. Wait. Give yourself time to think, calm down, and come up with a consciously thought-out plan of action. Except with young children, you always have the option to say to someone, "I'm too upset to respond to this right now. I need to calm down and think about it first."

Overcome Projection: The phenomenon of psychological projection causes parents to overreact to situations and their children's actions that trigger hurts, fears, and stressors from the parents' own pasts.

One example is a woman whose childhood background was laden with fear. She becomes a mother who is overly protective and smothering of her son because she is afraid something bad will happen to him. If she was overly criticized as a child and forced to do many chores, she may also have trouble saying "no" to him or asking him to help her because she is afraid he will feel the way she did as a child when she was criticized and forced to work. The projection interferes with her ability to parent effectively.

Another example is a father who angers easily and is overly controlling and intolerant of his children's behavior. Because he experienced excessive criticism and harsh punishment as a child, he was angry most of the time, but had no way to express it because of consequences from his parents if he did. The anger is stuck in him. So, when the emotion of anger is triggered in him by his children, at any level, the emotion overwhelms him and he loses his temper.

Because parents are so emotionally invested in their children, they also tend to regard their children's successes and failures as reflections of their own worth, Therefore, a parent who has low self-esteem (a self-fractured state), can overreact to what he or she perceives as a child's failure to perform in some way. An example of this would be a father who becomes unreasonably critical of his son when the son strikes out at a baseball game. The father experiences the son's failure to hit the ball as an attack on his own self-esteem and overreacts because of it.

At the very least, childhood abuse experiences and other traumatic childhood events can influence parenting styles in some unconscious emotionally reactive way. The phenomenon of projection can get in the way of clear-headed parenting.

Detach: The opposite of detachment is *attachment*. Melody Beattie in *Codependent No More* writes that "Attachment is becoming overly-involved, sometimes hopelessly entangled" (Beattie 1987, 52) with another's life and problems. She says that attachment can take many forms:

- We may become excessively worried about, and preoccupied with, a problem or person (our mental energy is attached).
- We may graduate to becoming obsessed with and controlling of the people and problems in our environment (our mental, physical, and emotional energy is directed at the object of our obsession).
- We may become reactive instead of acting authentically of our own volition (our mental, emotional, and physical energy is attached).
- We may become emotionally dependent on the people around us (now we're really attached).
- We may become caretakers (rescuers, enablers) to the people around us (firmly attaching ourselves to their need for us) (Ibid.).

Parents are emotionally involved with their children, as they should be, but being overly involved in a child's life because of over-attachment can cause a reactive environment to develop that is ongoing and inhibits the child from learning that he or she is self-capable. To balance the tendency to get overly involved with your child and to maintain self-focus as a parent, developing the skill of detachment can reduce reactive responses.

Determine Who Owns the Problem: Because parents get so emotionally involved with their children, they tend to take on their children's problems as their own. By detaching, a parent can gain a better perspective on who owns the problem, the child or the parent.

In *Parent Effectiveness Training (P.E.T.)*, Thomas Gordon writes:

A core concept in the P.E.T. model is the principle of problem ownership. Its importance cannot be overstated because so many parents fall into the trap of assuming responsibility for solving problems that their children own, rather than encouraging them to solve their problems themselves (Gordon, 2000, 30).

Encouraging children to solve their own problems teaches self-focus and encourages self-development.

Become Aware of How You Communicate with Your Children: No matter what the issue to be addressed or whether the parent or child owns the problem, the way you communicate with your child influences how things turn out. Automatic negative, reactive responses get you nowhere and drive you and your child apart. Consciously thought-out, self-directed responses can lead to progress and bring you together.

There are two parts to the communication process, speaking and listening. Often, parents overdo speaking and neglect listening. This creates resentment in children. Problems are perpetuated by speaking in ways that are harmful. Being critical and judgmental, competitive about who is right, and implementing *power over* techniques shut down communication. Listening opens it up.

When Your Child Has a Problem, Avoid Speaking in Ways that Hurt Rather than Help: Comments that are judgmental, order children about, threaten, or ridicule are always hurtful. When someone has a problem, giving advice, diverting away from the topic, and praising can also cause more harm than good, because the comments get in the way of a child learning to gain self-insight and to find a solution to his or her own problem. Of course, children need to be praised and advised. Parents teach, encourage, and guide all the time, but when a child has a specific problem to solve, these judgmental ways of communicating get in the way of the child's own problem-solving process.

Try Not to Make Your Child Wrong: We are all different. We think and reach conclusions in different ways and hold different values around what is important to us. What is important to a teenager may not be important to a parent and vice-versa. One thing that gets in the way of the parent/child relationship is that the parent tends to present his or her perspective as right and the child's as wrong. The result is that the parent negates what is important to the child. What works better is for the parent to provide the circumstances so that both parent and child feel free to present their differing perspectives without the fear of being judged. The conflict then becomes a puzzle that the parent and child try to resolve together.

Listen and Respond Reflectively: By listening and responding reflectively, you and your child can gain insight into a problem because, often, what your child presents to you as the problem rests on a deeper issue.

In *Parent Effectiveness Training*, Thomas Gordon presents a dialogue that he had with his teenage daughter. It illustrates how the safe emotional environment that is created through the reflective listening process can provide the opportunity for a child to get in touch with a troubling issue and gain insight around it. In this dialogue, it is not obvious at first that the child is bothered about something. The process of listening reflectively brings it out.

> Daughter: Daddy, what did you like in girls when you were a boy?
> Father: Sounds like you're wondering what you need in order to get boys to like you?
> Daughter: Yeah. For some reason they don't seem to like me and I don't know why.
> Father: You're confused why they don't seem to like you.
> Daughter: Well, I know I don't talk much. I'm afraid to talk in front of boys.
> Father: You just can't seem to open up and be relaxed with boys.
> Daughter: Yeah. I'm afraid I'll say something that will make me look silly.
> Father: You don't want them to think you're silly.
> Daughter: Yeah. So if I'm quiet, I don't even take that risk.
> Father: It seems safer to be quiet.
> Daughter: Yes, but that doesn't seem to get me anyplace, because now they must think I'm dull.
> Father: Being quiet doesn't get you what you want.
> Daughter: No. I guess you just have to take a chance (Gordon 2000, 91).

Gordon also writes:

Unusually coded messages that children send, particularly questions, often mean the child is coping with a deeper problem. Active [reflective] listening provides parents with a way of moving in and offering to help the child define the problem for herself, and starting up the process of problem solving *within the child*. Giving direct answers to these feelings-coded-as-questions almost invariably results in the parents muffing an opportunity to be an effective counselor on the real problem the child is grappling with (Gordon 2000, 91).

When the Parent Owns the Problem: If the child is doing something that annoys or upsets the parent, the parent owns the problem. Then the parent needs to figure out how to solve it. When you have a problem with your child, presenting it from the self-focused *I* position avoids making the child feel wrong. Once you have presented your problem, you can help your child process his or her reaction to it by listening and responding reflectively.

For example: After taking a shower, Mary, fourteen, usually leaves her dirty clothes and wet towel on the floor. Mom is sick of picking up after her.

Sample dialogue

Mom: I know it's hard for you to remember to pick up after a shower, but I get upset when I have to pick up the things left on the bathroom floor.

Mary: Sorry. I'll pick up them from now on.

The next time Mary takes a shower the clothes and towel are left on the floor.

Mom: (Holding the towel and clothes in front of her daughter.) These were on the floor again. What happened?

Mary: I forgot, but I'll remember next time.

Mom: Well, I need to take care of myself around this issue because I'm upset about it. Next time it happens, I think there needs to be a consequence.

Mary: I don't need a consequence. I'll remember.

Mom: Okay. I hear you saying that you don't need a consequence because you will remember next time, but I'm not sure that will happen. So, will you agree that if you forget again, there will be a consequence?

Mary: Okay.

Mom: I need to know what that consequence will be. Any suggestions?

Mary: Mmm…okay. If I forget, you can take my phone for the day.

Mom: Agreed.

This agreement, negotiated from a self-focused, nonreactive, inclusive perspective by Mom, is more likely to produce results than if she had said, "That's it! If you leave things on the bathroom floor one more time, I'm taking your phone!" Also, if Mary forgets, she has already agreed to the consequence because she suggested it.

Listen Silently: I first encountered the remarkable experiences that can happen when one listens silently to another when I was in graduate school in California. The Ojai Foundation was nearby. The concept of the way of council (when people sit in a circle, pass a talking piece, and listen to each other speak) evolved from the foundation's work. It was developed in the 1980s as an experimental process for dealing with the many cultural differences of the children who had immigrated to California and were attending a local junior high school. The school environment had become tense because of the differences and conflicts among the children. (More than thirty different cultures and different points of view were represented) The council process was implemented so children could tell the stories of their backgrounds and their problems. While one child held the talking piece and spoke, the others listened silently. Through the experiment, educators learned that when children sat in council with each other in the classroom, from a young age on, rather than gangs developing that pit one faction against another, the children came to know each other as individuals. Difficulties between children were worked out during the council process, and the differences between them fell away. Since the tragedy of Columbine and other school shootings, more and more schools are adopting the way of council into their curriculums to promote understanding and relatedness and avoid conflict and tragedy.

The book, *The Way of Council,* is about the process. Just as it works in schools to promote understanding and relatedness, the way of council works in families. The Ojai Foundation offers seminars and retreats for teachers, parents, counselors, corporate administrators, and people from all walks of life. A gift parents and teachers can give children is to learn the techniques and then to sit in council with them at home and in school.

The Way of Council website is at: *ojaifoundation.org.*

Find Solutions that Work for All: Given the opportunity to participate in the process of solving a problem, a child often comes up with surprisingly insightful and fair solutions. By being included in the problem-solving process, the child gains power and self-influence on the outcome. This encourages cooperation. When a conflict arises, whether between parent and child, or siblings, the conflict resolution process calls for each person involved to brainstorm possible solutions and write them down. Then the solutions that are not acceptable to all parties are crossed out.

The ones that are agreed to are used to solve the problem. As problems reoccur, the brainstorming process is repeated (Gordon, 2000).

Power Over as a Last Resort: If nothing else works and a problem cannot be solved through cooperative effort and mutual understanding, then it's time to set a firm parental power over boundary. This is a last resort tactic because, instead of bringing parent and child together, it can drive them apart.

The first step in setting a boundary is to validate the other person's position. For instance, in the dialogue between Mom and Mary about leaving clothes on the bathroom floor, Mom started the boundary-setting process by validating Mary's point of view, saying to her, "I know it's hard for you to remember to pick up your things after a shower." Having said this, Mom continued unfolding the boundary-making process with a self-focused *I* message, "But I'm upset that I'm left to pick up things left on the bathroom floor." She gave Mary another chance to comply with her request that Mary pick up after herself. When Mary failed again, Mom set the boundary and negotiated the consequence that would happen if Mary forgot again.

In this instance, Mary cooperated with her mother around the boundary Mom set, agreeing to the consequence. Other scenarios may not turn out so well. When a child refuses to cooperate in the boundary setting process, the last resort is to establish power over limits; then the parent alone sets the boundary and the consequence. Unfortunately, this usually results in more resistance from the child and more tension between parent and child. This is why setting a power over boundary that has not been negotiated is used as a last resort.

The Couple Relationship: Pitfalls and Traps: The kind of emotional climate that develops in a couple relationship determines whether children feel emotionally safe and secure or emotionally unsafe and fearful. Overall, the more children feel free to be themselves, age appropriately and with appropriate containment of actions and behavior, the more pleasant the environment, and the greater chance that the self-esteem of each child will thrive.

Creating such a safe emotional environment usually requires conscious effort on the part of parents around the pitfalls and traps that ensnare couples and produce reactive emotional responses. Working at maintaining self-focus with each other, being aware of projective

responses, the differences between men and women, how different personality types perceive things, and detaching when necessary will contribute to creating a safer emotional environment for your children.

Assess Your Family for Its Underlying Structural Dynamics: The
parents set the stage for how family dynamics play out. The healthy structure of a family depends upon the parents' ability to maintain self-focus
with each other and the children, their conscious awareness of what is
going on, their capacity for effective couple communication, and their
joint determination to create a safe emotional environment for all, while
at the same time, providing containment around children's behavior.

Salvador Minuchin and Murray Bowen have created concepts and
terms for determining when family structures are off. Red flags that indicate problems are triangles that exist among family members, cross-generational coalitions, diffuse or rigid boundaries, lack of self-focus (too
much emotional reactivity) among family members, deflection of the
couple's problems onto the children or one child, and unresolved family
problems that get passed on from one generation to another. Once you
have assessed your family's structure, you can start addressing problem
areas in order to bring about second order change.

The next section, VI, is devoted to identifying personality type preferences. Learning your type is a tool for self understanding. Learning
the personality types of others is a way to understand them. The subject is addressed briefly here as it relates to psychological development in
children.

Personality Type Development in Children: We all want to be appreciated for who we are. If, as children, our parents communicate that appreciation, we internalize it and appreciate ourselves (Nichols and Schwartz,
1998). Praising a child for what he or she does is one way of communicating appreciation. However, by understanding your child's typology, you
gain the opportunity to appreciate who your child is.

As parents, we focus on what our children do rather than on how they
choose to function and interpret the world as directed from inside them
(Kiersy and Bates, 1984). By discerning a child's typology, a parent can validate natural inclinations and strengths, as well as provide opportunities
for developing them. Problems occur when a child's personality typology

is different from the parents' and is not valued. Then the parents may try to change the child's natural and preferred way of functioning to their own.

For instance, extraversion vs. introversion: Extraverts are energized by being around people. They are social and action oriented and adapt easily. They make up the majority of the population in our culture. Introverts, on the other hand, focus inward more to the world of ideas and the imagination. Being around people drains their energy. They are not outgoing or easily sociable. They don't speak up or adapt easily. To re-energize, they need to spend time alone. Introverts are in the minority in our culture. Extraverted children are better adapted to the school environment than introverts, who can feel overwhelmed and lost there.

You can guess that your child is probably an extravert if he or she loves being with people and trying new things, is in the middle of activities, and is comfortable in a crowded room. If your child plays imaginatively for long periods, seeks quiet activity after school to re-energize and sits on the sidelines and is quiet in a crowd, he or she is probably an introvert.

In our culture, extraversion is appreciated more than introversion. The concern here, especially for introverts, is that children whose type preferences are not appreciated and validated do not have the opportunity to develop their natural skills and talents, so have a hard time becoming authentically themselves as adults.

> In normal type development, a child regularly uses the preferred process…and becomes increasingly skillful in its use. More and more able to control the favorite process, the child acquires the traits that belong to it. Thus the child's type is determined by the process that is used, trusted, and developed most (Myers and Myers, 1980, 173).

From the perspective of self psychology, a child whose typology preferences are recognized, validated, and encouraged early on can be off to a good start in life because children gain confidence and self-assurance by building on their strengths. Children who are made to be extraverts when they are, in fact, introverts, or vice-versa, are constantly frustrated because they are not naturally good at what they are expected to do. Over time, this becomes a self-fracturing experience—with loss of confidence and self-esteem. By gaining a good sense of oneself in childhood through encouragement of type preferences, the individual gets the chance to work out who he or she is authentically designed to be, and then to build upon that throughout life by expanding one's repertoire of competencies.

Section VI presents personality typology theory, as well as reference material for determining your own type and how it interacts with others. Learning your typology can allow you to accept who you are without being defensive, and it gives you the insight to accept others as they are as well.

VI

Know Yourself

31 • Understanding Personality Types

By learning about one's type, an individual can realize his or her personality style, accommodate it, and live more authentically in the outer world. Carl Jung, a psychiatrist who practiced his profession in the first half of the twentieth century, is credited with defining the concept of personality types. Today many psychologists accept that there are sixteen basic types and that, like right-handedness and left-handedness, one's typology is inherited and inborn.

Jung created his system of typology, not to classify people into categories, but to give himself a system for examining the human mind, a starting point for comparing and contrasting human behavior. His typology system is a tool for sorting out how individuals think. It provides a practical way to gain insight into how you prefer to function in the world—how you prefer to process inner and outer experiences, and how you present yourself to others. Yet a human being is much more complex than the differences that can be sorted out in a personality classification system. The personality types are presented here to offer insight into the psychological complexity of human nature, your own and that of others.

Getting a sense of your typology preferences can be achieved by examining these questions:

1. Where do I prefer to focus my attention—on the outside world or the one within my mind?

2. How do I acquire information? Do I rely more on what my five senses tell me is true or do I follow my intuition?

3. How do I process information, make decisions, reach conclusions, form opinions? Am I most influenced by what seems rational and logical, or does how I feel about something influence me more?

4. How do I relate to and choose to function in the outer world? Do I like to control the day by planning it (maybe making a list) and getting things done or am I more spontaneous about what I do, seeking to let the day come to me by seeing what happens (Myers 1962).

According to Jung's definition of personality types, and the later work of Isabel Myers and Katherine Briggs, who created the Myers-Briggs Type Indicator (a test for identifying one's type), four scales that measure personality preferences determine typology. They are Extraversion vs. Introversion, Sensation vs. Intuition, Thinking vs. Feeling, and Judging vs. Perceiving. Determining where you are on the four scales can help you understand yourself, why you do what you do, and why you are good at some things and not others. And understanding how different personality types prefer to function will give you insight into why others act as they do and why you have misunderstandings and arguments with others that leave you bewildered and thinking, *How can he or she think that way, feel that way, reach that conclusion? Why can't this person understand what I'm talking about, accept what I am saying?*

Taking the Myers-Briggs Type Indicator test will show you where you fall on each scale. For example, it will tell you how extraverted or introverted you are by determining how close or how far you score from the center. A person perfectly balanced between extraversion and introversion would score exactly in the center, but no one is perfectly balanced. We all have a preference. You can determine your general typology, though, and gain insight into yourself and others without taking the test by becoming familiar with the concepts and terms and by deciding on your preferences. Here are descriptions of the terms that describe the types.

Extraversion/Introversion

Extraverts prefer to direct their energy out into the world because they are most interested in the outer world of people and things rather than the inner one of ideas, concepts, and the imagination. They are action-oriented. The great majority of people in our culture (about seventy-five percent) are extraverted. Because of where they focus their attention, extraverts are more aware of what goes on in their external environment than introverts. Extraverts are usually sociable, outgoing, friendly, and good at casual conversation because they think on their feet while talking. They adapt easily and like to explore new environments and meet new people. In a group discussion, extraverts are usually quick thinkers who jump into the conversation without hesitation. They enjoy being in social settings because being with people charges their batteries. They feel lonely when alone. They choose to have a broad range of experiences and friends.

Introverts prefer to direct their energy inward to the world of ideas, concepts, and imagination. They are thought-oriented. Being in social settings with many people drains their energy. About twenty-five percent of our population is introverted. They are not outgoing, are hesitant in new situations, and have a hard time speaking up quickly because they need to think about what they want to say first. In a group discussion or argument with someone, often they don't get much chance to speak because their thinking process takes too long. By the time they are ready to say something, someone else is already talking. They prefer familiar settings, don't adapt easily because they are most comfortable in their own space, and tend to want to guard it from intrusions. They prefer being alone, with a trusted partner, or with a small group of friends. They seek deep meaningful relationships, so are not good at small talk. They can feel isolated in the presence of others and can have a hard time feeling like they fit in. Introverts need to be alone to recharge and so are more comfortable alone than extraverts. They prefer depth of experience, rather than breadth (Kiersey and Bates 1984).

Extraverts can deal with the inner world of ideas and concepts when called upon to do so, and introverts deal with the world around them when necessary. We all do both, no matter what our preference. How well an extravert can do introverted processes and how well an introvert can do extraverted functions depends on how close to the middle one falls on the Extraversion-Introversion scale.

Sensation/Intuition

Like the Extraversion/Introversion scale, where you fall on the Sensation/Intuition scale also determines a preference for focusing on the outer or inner worlds. However, where the Extroversion/Introversion scale measures where you prefer to focus your attention, the Sensation/Intuition scale measures how you acquire information, either by how you are informed from without by your five senses or how you are informed from within, intuitively.

Sensate people prefer to rely primarily on their five senses for acquiring information. Their eyes, ears, taste and senses of smell and touch inform them about reality. They live in the present and are action-oriented. Most are good at following directions, especially when putting something together. They like to become skilled at doing something and then keep doing it. They notice and remember details, are practical and realistic, and have the ability to stay focused on what they are doing in the outer world and on what is going on around them. Approximately seventy-five percent of the population prefers to rely primarily on the five senses to acquire information.

Intuitives rely on their five senses, but also seem to be informed by an interior knowing—a hunch, gut feeling, sixth sense. They are thought-oriented, instead of action-oriented. Rather than being focused in the present, they are more drawn to a future perspective, because they like to think about what is possible rather than what is. They think conceptually, rather than specifically. Therefore, strong intuitives can have trouble paying attention to details and can lose track of what they are doing in the outer world, because they become so preoccupied by the inner one. They can be forgetful, lose things, have trouble memorizing factual detailed information, and can walk into a room and forget what they were going to do there. Most intuitives do not follow directions well. Extremely intuitive people can become impractical daydreamers.

Intuitives like to learn new things and put ideas together to form a new concept or way of thinking, but once they have mastered or created something, they may lose interest and have trouble with the practical aspect of follow-through. Their talent is that they can be great innovators. They are the original thinkers in the world. Many are writers, artists, researchers, scientists, teachers, psychologists, and talented innovators with computers. Their intuitive way of thinking is insightful, can be profound, and can lead to new discoveries about the world and the mind. And deeply intuitive people often have psychic abilities. Approximately twenty-five percent of the population prefers to acquire information intuitively.

We all use both our senses and intuition to acquire information. How much you use one over the other depends on how close you fall to the middle of the sensation vs. intuition scale.

Thinking/Feeling

Various sources report that this is the only scale that seems to have a gender bias. About sixty-five percent of men are thinkers and about sixty-five percent of women are feelers. Although the majority of men are thinkers and the majority of women are feelers, approximately thirty-five percent of men are feelers and thirty-five percent of women are thinkers. Therefore, it is important to keep in mind that the stereotypical characteristics of men as logical and rational and women as emotional, does not hold true for feeling men and thinking women.

Thinkers tend to follow a detached method of coming to conclusions. They are comfortable and skilled at reaching decisions based on impersonal logic, the facts. They do well with organizing ideas and facts without regard to emotional input. Things are black and white to strong thinkers, logical and obvious. Thinkers feel free to express their points of view, because they don't get overly involved in how another will react to what is said. Strong thinkers do not worry much about hurting someone's feelings, and they don't take things as personally as feelers do. What a feeler may interpret as an uncaring critical statement by the thinking speaker, the thinker regards as a logical account of the situation. Thinkers are much better at saying "yes" when they want to say "yes," and "no" when they want to say "no," because they don't have the problem of over-empathizing with how the other will react to "no." Because of this, they have more capacity to say "yes" or "no" based on how they want to respond, and that is what logically makes sense to them. In personal relationships, thinkers get frustrated with feelers because thinkers regard them as too emotional, indirect, illogical, their thinking process too muddled. However, strong thinkers run the risk of becoming so detached from their own and another's feelings that disconnection from oneself and the other can occur. The relationship with the other can suffer as a result, and the thinker can become emotionally shut down and isolated.

The feeler's reasoning process for reaching conclusions is based on personal values—what feels right. Issues are not black and white for feelers, because they have to consider mitigating circumstances before reaching a conclusion. Emotions play a significant role in how feelers function. As parents, thinkers can be fair consistent disciplinarians with their children, because they follow a rational detached approach. Feelers have problems with consistency, because they become overly involved emotionally and can be swayed by a child's perspective and pleading.

However, thinkers who are too detached from their children and feelers who are too emotionally involved can both create significant psychological problems for their children. Balance is best.

Feelers are empathic. Empathy, the ability to put oneself in the other's place to imagine how he or she is feeling, is a good thing. This ability enables feelers to be good at managing personal relationships. Being overly empathic, though, creates problems for feelers. Because they are so empathic, they feel compelled to put themselves in the other's place and assess the impact on the other person of what they want to say. This automatic process, in effect, shuts them up. They cannot say what they want to say because they feel too guilty about how the other will feel when they say it. And there is another aspect here that is a problem for the feeler. Because the thinker is such a direct communicator, the feeler is afraid the thinker will respond to what is said in a way that will hurt the feeler's feelings. This worry also shuts them up. The feeler becomes tongue-tied. This creates more problems for the feeler, because he or she then becomes resentful and angry with what the feeler regards as the insensitive thinker's way of doing things. This cycle goes on and on. The relationship suffers as a result.

We all use both logic and feelings to reach conclusions. How much you prefer one process over the other depends upon how close to the middle you fall on the Thinking/Feeling scale. If you are a thinker who feels that your life is too logically driven, then developing your emotional side will bring you to a happier, more balanced place in life. If you are a feeler who is overwhelmed by emotions, using the coping skills mentioned previously (which are based on using your thinking function), will help you to calm down, think more clearly, and gain a better perspective.

Judging/Perceiving

Judging here does not mean being judgmental. Rather the term refers to someone who needs to come to conclusions about things, wants life ordered and predictable, needs closure. Judgers like to make lists, follow them, and cross tasks off as they are completed. They are careful planners and do not like things left up in the air.

Judging types feel restless and unsettled until a decision is made, a task completed. When they are working on something, they do not like to be interrupted. They have trouble going with the flow. They set deadlines and are serious about meeting them. They are good at follow-through and completing tasks. Judgers value work over play and like to be in control.

Perceivers like to keep their options open and be spontaneous. They resist making plans. Perceivers have trouble committing to a course of action because they fear something better might come along that they had not considered. They do not value meeting goals the way judgers do, so are more casual in their attitude toward accomplishing something. They can be procrastinators. They are less conscious of time than judgers and can miss deadlines and appointments. Perceivers value play over work and want to be free.

How uptight you get when tasks are not completed and situations resolved (judgers), or how anxious you get when deadlines and obligations make you feel hemmed in (perceivers) depends on where you fall on the Judging/Perceiving scale. An overly judging personality whose life has become too serious can be brought into balance by seeking to be spontaneous and to have more fun. An overly perceiving personality whose life has become chaotic through lack of planning and attention to details can be brought into balance by becoming more disciplined.

In summary: Intuitive types are motivated by inner guiding principles, inspiration, possibilities. Sensing types are motivated by facts, details, what is. Feeling types are motivated by an inner system of values based on feeling. Thinking types are motivated by reaching logical conclusions. How these perspectives are used as the individual goes through life depends on either an outer focus on things and people (extraversion) or an inner focus on ideas (introversion) and whether one likes life to unfold in an organized controlled way (judging) or an open-ended way that promotes freedom from restraint (perceiving).

Here are the four personality typology scales. Can you estimate where you fall on each scale?

Extraversion_____*_____**Introversion**

Sensation _____*_____**Intuition**

Thinking_____*_____**Feeling**

Judging_____*_____**Perceiving**

Typology traits are abbreviated in the following way: Extroversion is **E**; Introversion, **I**; Sensation **S**; Intuition **N**; Thinking **T**; Feeling **F**; Judging **J** and Perception **P**. Example: An introverted, intuitive, feeling, perceiver would be an **INFP**.

Once you have estimated your personality type, you can find a brief description of it in the next chapter entitled *Determining Typology*. The descriptions are organized into four groups according to the first two letters of each type. The four extraverted sensate (ES) types are described first, page 105. Next are the four extraverted intuitives (EN), page 111. Third are the introverted sensates (IS), page 116. Last are the four introverted intuitive (IN) types, page 121.

For a more complete description of the types, there are books specifically focused on this topic, including *Personality Types* by Daryl Sharp, *Gifts Differing* by Isabel Briggs Myers with Peter B. Myers, *Just Your Type* by Paul C. Tieger and Barbara Barron-Tieger, and *Please Understand Me* by David Kiersey and Marilyn Bates. Also, you can determine exactly where you fall on each scale and get feedback on your personality type by taking the Myers-Briggs Type Indicator free online. Just type in "Myers Briggs test," and it will come up.

GROUP ONE
The Extraverted Sensate Types: ESTJ, ESTP, ESFJ, ESFP

Of the sixteen personality types, these four, ESTJ, ESTP, ESFJ, and ESFP, make up the largest typology group in the United States—more than fifty percent of the population. If you prefer and predominantly use extraversion and sensation, then you are in synch with our society. Because extraverted sensate people make up the majority, they have the most influence on advertising strategies, corporate hierarchies, how our educational systems function, how media content is presented, and what the most commonly accepted values are in our society. People with these typology traits are likely to have their strengths validated as children and adults, because they will interact with like-minded people as they move through life. What they do well will probably be rewarded by approval, good grades in school, and financial success. The exception can be the perceivers (P) who have a more difficult time with follow-through, staying on task, and disciplining themselves to study. Extraverted sensate people are practical doers who are animated through interactions with the outer world and people. They effectively interact with others, and are talented at absorbing and paying attention to facts.

Extraverted sensates are attracted to outer experiences that excite sensations—sights, sounds, tastes, touches, and smells. Because they are focused on the external world of people and things, they may have difficulty valuing or relating to concepts that are not concrete, that are based on introverted and intuitive skills. Therefore, some extraverted sensate people [thinkers] may not be interested in or focus on how another thinks and feels inside (Sharp 1987). This can create relationship difficulties and misunderstandings. Extraverted sensates may also be disconnected from their own inner worlds of intuitive wisdom and guidance.

Here are the ES types:

ESTJ

ESTJs favor extraversion, sensation, thinking, and judging preferences. They are decisive and responsible directors who make up approximately fifteen percent of the population. Their strength is thinking, weakness feeling. "This is perhaps the most traditionally masculine type and includes more men than any other" (Myers and Myers 1995, 87).

ESTJs are outgoing and friendly. They make decisions quickly based on impersonal facts, details, logical analysis, and reasoning. They are leaders. At work, they are good project managers. ESTJs are competitive, hardworking, assertive, responsible, practical, and thorough. They value order, accuracy, routines, conformity, and established ethical standards based on factual information. They like organized settings that are predictable, and value being useful, steadfast, and dutiful.

ESTJs are focused in the present and are aware of what is going on in their surroundings. They like to create rules and procedures that order and organize their professional and family lives. They are effective in supervisory and leadership roles that evaluate and direct others. They prefer to be in control following established rules that are based on logic. They are uncomfortable with abstract theories, inefficiency, confusion, change. They work to achieve an end or product. ESTJs like to be appreciated and recognized for the results of their efforts (Kiersey and Bates 1984.).

Occupational preferences: ESTJs like positions that deal with people, details, facts, analysis, and things. They choose careers in finance, production, construction, law, mechanics, business, industry, project management, administration, medicine, and education (Myers and Myers 1995).

Challenges: Because they live in the here and now, ESTJs like to make decisions quickly and move on. Therefore, they can reach conclusions prematurely without careful consideration of all that needs to be addressed. Consequences in the future can result. They can be negative, sarcastic, and impatient. Also, ESTJs need to develop empathy around how their actions impact others' feelings and points of view. Because they like to decide quickly, establish rules, and follow them, they may over-control people and situations, which creates resentment in others. And ESTJs' need for predictable structure and their resistance to change can cause them to be too rigid and stubborn when compromise is needed. Because they make decisions based on logical conclusions, rather than feeling values, they can be too unyielding in the face of another's point of view, especially if that point of view is based on how the other feels. ESTJs can be impatient, intolerant, judgmental, and can be overly assertive and intimidating when expressing themselves. Relationships can suffer as a result.

ESTJs can benefit from working to develop their weakest function, feeling, to become more aware and value their own feelings and those of others.

ESTP

ESTPs favor extraversion, sensation, thinking, and perceiving preferences. They are fun-loving risk takers. They live in the moment and make up approximately thirteen percent of the population. Their strength is sensation, weakness intuition. ESTPs like to be the life of the party.

They value freedom, action, excitement, and adventure. They are outgoing, friendly, good-natured, cheerful, optimistic, and talkative. Enthusiastic, clever, funny, and charming, they enjoy fun and material possessions. ESTPs like physical activity and the outdoors, and are usually good at sports. Practical, adaptable, realistic, resourceful, open-minded, and tolerant, they are good at negotiating and getting people to compromise and cooperate. They are capable of absorbing many facts, but learn best with concrete hands-on experience. ESTPs are good at in-the-moment problem solving that is based on logic, facts, and first-hand knowledge. They work well with machinery, tools, and materials. They make decisions based on factual information and logic rather than feeling values. They are observant and aware of what is going on around them, and they like sensate experiences. ESTPs are process-oriented rather than results-oriented; that is, they enjoy doing something for the sake of doing it rather than for the results to be achieved.

Occupational preferences: They are attracted to technology, business, industry, production, construction, accounting, banking, culinary arts, jobs in recreation, marketing, health, and other practical hands-on professions. ESTPs are skilled at trouble-shooting on the job and assessing the reality of a situation to negotiate a solution. They meet crises well. They like jobs that provide action and freedom.

Challenges: ESTPs may have trouble with impulsive behavior that brings on unwanted consequences, and difficulties with commitment, follow-through, long range planning, self-discipline, schoolwork, and addressing tense or serious personal issues. They may be dissatisfied with the status quo and want change.

ESTPs can benefit from developing their weakest function, intuition. The skill of thinking intuitively is one of using the imagination to see the overall picture, the patterns of connection that indicate how what happens in the future is the result of what happens now. It is future-oriented. Intuitive thinking is a slower reflective process that can moderate action-oriented, in-the-moment impulsive behavior that might lead to unwanted outcomes.

ESFJ

ESFJs favor extraversion, sensation, feeling, and judging preferences. Harmony in relationships is most important. They enjoy sociability and traditions and make up approximately fourteen percent of the population. Their strength is feeling, weakness thinking. ESFJs are devoted to family and friends.

Sympathetic, outgoing, generous, and friendly, ESFJs enjoy entertaining in social settings and experiencing the warmth and fellowship of others. They are cooperative, conscientious, hardworking, responsible, and productive. ESFJs think best while speaking and gain pleasure from being useful. They like to provide stability. They value supporting traditions, routines, and right actions, and make decisions based on feeling values rather than thinking. ESFJs are practical, realistic, neat, accurate, and like to save and conserve. They prefer hands-on experiences and want things scheduled and settled rather than open-ended. They are loyal supporters of home life, the community, and the workplace. ESFJs are black and white in their thinking about values—something is clearly either right or wrong. They like to work to achieve an end or produce a product. They like being recognized and appreciated for the results of their efforts (Kiersey and Bates 1984).

Occupational preferences: They are found in business, teaching, the ministry, nursing, and care-giving health professions. ESFJs are excellent at sales, as managers, and administrators. They like occupations that provide service to others.

Challenges: Because of their strong judgmental stance around values, they may want to impose these values on others, which can produce resentment. ESFJs are easily hurt and overly sensitive to criticism. They can take things too personally and be emotionally reactive. Also, over-sensitivity to others' needs can cause them to become too involved with others' problems and care-giving. They may have difficulty saying "no" and setting boundaries, be overwhelmed by their own emotional state and by too much commitment to others. They may have too much responsibility in their lives and not enough fun. ESFJs can also have difficulty with changes in plans, interruptions, disorder, and making decisions based on logic. They may not be good at dealing with abstract ideas and impersonal analysis.

ESFJs can benefit by developing their weakest function, thinking, especially when upset. The coping skills presented earlier develop the thinking function: "Live in the Moment," "Don't Say 'Yes' When You Want to Say 'No,'" "Quiet the Negative, Fearful, Worrying Voice," "Overcome Projection," and "Detach."

If you are a strong feeler, that does not mean you are not good at thinking when it comes to impersonal work like learning something new, studying, or handling a job. What it does mean is that how you function in relationship to others and how you personally experience what goes on in your life is based more on feeling values than on rational logical thought. Because of this, you can become overwhelmed emotionally in many situations. Developing the rational, analytical, and logical thinking function can help to moderate this tendency.

ESFP

ESFPs favor extraversion, sensation, feeling, and perceiving preferences. They like to perform, are good company, generous, and make up approximately thirteen percent of the population. Their strength is sensation, weakness intuition. They are happiest in the spotlight.

ESFPs are entertaining, friendly, and sympathetic. They are good at addressing practical, concrete problems, and conflict resolution in the workplace and social settings. They are adaptable, accepting of people and situations, realistic, and tolerant. Like other sensate types, they are aware of what is going on in their surroundings. Enthusiastic, curious, helpful, compassionate, they are tactful, open-minded, optimistic, and fun-loving. ESFPs like surprises, action, excitement, material possessions, fashion, beauty, pleasure, and having options. They prefer to be with others rather than alone. They learn best by doing rather than by studying books, and may not be good at processing abstract concepts. They are good at coping with unexpected changes and enjoy physical activities, sports, and the outdoors.

Occupational preferences: ESFPs like action-oriented careers with people: sales, entertainment, public relations, business, education, nursing, working with people in crisis. They prefer jobs that vary activities during the day.

Challenges: ESFPs can become overly involved with others' problems and have difficulty setting boundaries in relationships. They can have trouble disciplining their children because they can be overly sympathetic and want to avoid stressful situations and conflict. Because they love fun, play, and excitement, they may overlook responsibilities in pursuit of what they want to do. Process-oriented rather than results-oriented, they enjoy doing something for the sake of doing it rather than the results to be achieved. (Kiersey and Bates 1984).

Although they do well with conflict resolution in the workplace and social situations, they avoid conflict in personal relationships. ESFPs do not like to reveal their deep feelings and avoid confrontations and anxious personal situations rather than dealing with them. This creates resentment in others. Since they live in the moment, it is not easy for them to contemplate how their present actions will impact their future well-being. They can become easily bored and too impulsive in their actions. ESFPs can benefit, therefore, by developing their weakest typology skill, intuition. The intuitive function uses the imagination to consider the overall picture, the patterns of connection that indicate how present actions lead to future developments. In the case of the ESFP, who prefers fun and excitement over responsibility and escape over dealing with stressful situations, developing intuitive abilities to influence future outcomes is the challenge.

GROUP TWO
The Extraverted Intuitive Types: ENTJ, ENTP, ENFJ, ENFP

The descriptions of the personality types in GROUP ONE (ES types, the extraverted sensates) explain that extraverted people focus the majority of their attention on the outer world of people and things. The extraverted sensate is gifted at being aware of what is going on in the here and now and acting on it. GROUP TWO examines how extraverted intuitives interact with the world. As the extraverted sensate focuses on the here and now and acts on it, the extraverted intuitive looks beyond people and objects in the here and now and imagines what they can become, what is possible.

Daryl Sharp, a Jungian analyst from Toronto, writes in *Personality Types*, "The primary purpose of intuition is to perceive aspects of the world that are not apprehended by other functions. Intuition is like a sixth sense that 'sees' something not actually there" (Sharp, 1987, 59). He goes on to say that if an extraverted sensate and an extraverted intuitive were to enter an old empty house together, they would see it in different ways:

> The sensate type sees the bare walls, the shabby window casements, the dirty floors. The intuitive sees rather what can be done with the space—the walls painted in soft pastels, pictures in place, sanded and shiny floors, clean windows and curtains, even where the furniture will go.

> Sensation types see only what is in front of them. Intuitives see the same scene transformed, as if in an inner vision, as if the house were already furnished and completely redecorated. None of this is available to the sensation function, which sees what is there at that moment in time. Hence, the sensation type is well advised to bring along an intuitive when shopping for a house. Naturally the opposite is also true, for while the intuitive is spellbound by the possibilities, the sensation type notices whether damp is seeping into the basement, the state of the plumbing, the number of electrical plugs, the distance to the nearest school, and so on (Sharp 1987, 60-61).

Where one type does well with analyzing the situation as it is, the other does well with imagining what can be. However, the sensate may reject the house because he or she cannot imagine the future possibilities; the intuitive may buy the house without having a realistic understanding of how much work and money it will take to restore it.

Here are the EN types:

ENTJ

ENTJs favor extraversion, intuition, thinking, and judging preferences. They are forceful leaders who take charge and like power. Approximately four percent of the population is this type. Their strength is thinking, weakness feeling. "ENTJ people use their thinking to run as much of the world as may be theirs to run" (Myers and Myers 1995, 85).

They value intelligence and competency in themselves and others. They have a future focus, are visionary and gifted long-range planners. ENTJs enjoy the process of organizing projects, ideas, people, situations, complex challenges, and executive action. They are well-spoken, quick decision makers, and direct communicators. ENTJs like structure and clear guidelines for directing the behavior of themselves and others. They are drawn to complex theories and ideas, big far-reaching projects, and they meet deadlines well. Strong-willed and opinionated, they value efficiency, honesty, right action, self-expertise, consistency, and rules. Often career driven, they like learning, action, and hard work, and admire power gained through competency. ENTJs dislike inefficiency, incompetence, and redundancy. They have high expectations of themselves and others. They value recognition for their capabilities, competency, and ideas.

Occupational preferences: ENTJs strive to be in-charge leaders no matter what profession they choose. They are strategic planners who are generally drawn to working in structured organizations where their logical, analytical, and administrative skills are valued. They seek careers as corporate executives, administrators, and managers, lawyers, university professors, financial managers, scientists, engineers, and entrepreneurs.

Challenges: ENTJs can be impatient, insensitive, intimidating, critical, and so driven by rules and logic that they overlook feelings, their own and others'. They can be easily irritated by what others do, especially when what they do does not make sense to the ENTJ or does not meet their standards. ENTJs can make decisions too quickly without paying attention to details and others' perspectives. They may be stubborn about making changes when change is needed because, for ENTJs, guidelines and rules direct behavior. In order to change behavior, first they have to change the rules. Also, because of their career driven focus, they may overlook tending to personal and family life.

ENTJs can benefit from developing their weakest function, feeling, to become more aware of their own feeling values and those of others.

ENTP

ENTPs favor extraversion, intuition, thinking, and perceiving preferences. They have a strong creative drive. Innovative, they follow their own ideas and inspirations with passion. ENTPs make up approximately five percent of the population. Their strength is intuition, weakness sensation. They are drawn to what can be.

ENTPs are focused on the future. They are versatile original thinkers and can be leaders because they are skilled communicators, good at motivating others and negotiating. They are confident and convincing. They are charming and friendly individuals who are independent, adaptable, easy-going, and funny. ENTPs have many interests and are adventurous with ideas. They value innovation, ingenuity, improvisation, debate for the challenge and fun of it, new possibilities and ideas, new undertakings and projects. Imaginative, they gain satisfaction from others listening to, understanding, and appreciating their ideas. Open, flexible, enthusiastic, and outgoing by nature, ENTPs are curious, clever, entertaining, and tolerant. They are not critical of others. They like interesting conversation, puns, having options, troubleshooting on the spot, gaining the upper hand, challenges, and complexity. They dislike tending to details, follow-through, daily tasks and routines, the mundane, the ordinary, the standard traditional way, conformity, and jobs without innovative challenges. ENTPs value others recognizing their capabilities and competencies (Kiersey and Bates, 1984).

Occupational preferences: They like jobs that provide one challenge after another—entrepreneurs, scientists, troubleshooters, politicians. ENTPs seek careers in business, sales, education, mechanics, psychology, industry, social work, and other professions with ongoing opportunities to be innovative or start new projects.

Challenges: ENTPs can have difficulty finishing a project once the creative part is over, and with following through on commitments. They may want to keep options open when a decision is needed. They can be impulsive and have difficulty following routines. They can be stubborn about doing necessary things that they do not want to do. Life can become a series of unfinished projects (Myers and Myers 1980).

ENTPs can benefit by paying attention to what is happening in the here and now and by developing their weakest function, sensation. Using the sensation function encourages attention to details like tending to the routine tasks of daily living—paying bills, housekeeping, and finishing projects. With this effort, their lives can become more productive, stable, and stress free.

ENFJ

ENFJs favor extraversion, intuition, feeling, and judging preferences. They seek harmony, are charismatic leaders and eager to please others. They make up approximately five percent of the population. Their strength is feeling, weakness thinking. ENFJs "value, above all, harmonious human contacts" (Kiersey and Bates 1984, 106).

ENFJs express themselves well when speaking and do very well in social situations because they are warm, generous, and kind. They cooperate, conform, and are trustworthy, reliable, and tolerant. As leaders, they like to organize situations and plan events. They have a future focus, and are insightful and curious about ideas and academic subjects. They are good at encouraging others to do their best. ENFJs are empathic, not critical. They listen to others well. Since they are nurturing and loyal, harmonious family and home lives are high priorities. ENFJs like having things organized and settled. They value being recognized and appreciated for what they contribute to the welfare of others (Kiersey and Bates 1984).

Occupational preferences: ENFJs do well in positions where they work with others in a cooperative effort, either as leaders or followers, because they perform equally well in either role. Careers in education, psychology, entertainment, business, sales, social work, religion, and other jobs where their people to people skills are utilized suit them.

Challenges: ENFJs can develop such a strong feeling function that they become ruled by their emotions—too empathic, sympathetic, and easily hurt. They can have difficulty setting boundaries with others, saying "yes" when they want to say "no," and can be overwhelmed with too many responsibilities because of care-giving to others. ENFJs are so good-natured and concerned with the well being of others that others take advantage of them. The result can be that they sacrifice their own needs and well being for the sake of harmony with others. They can also have trouble reaching decisions based on logic rather than feeling values. (Tieger and Barron-Tieger 2000).

ENFJs can benefit from developing their weakest function, thinking. By using thinking, they can balance their tendency to be too emotional. By practicing coping skills that rely on conscious thinking like "Live in the Moment," "Don't Say 'Yes' When You Want to Say 'No,'" and "Detach," they can keep themselves on a more even keel emotionally.

ENFP

ENFPs favor extraversion, intuition, feeling, and perceiving preferences. They are inspired, insightful, seekers of meaning, and motivated by an undeniable, innovative, creative drive. Approximately five percent of the population is ENFP. Their strength is intuition, weakness sensation. ENFPs "value inspiration above anything else" (Myers and Myers, 1995, 106).

Enthusiastic, passionate, optimistic, especially with other people about their own ideas, ENFPs enjoy imagining and initiating new projects based on those ideas. They have less interest in follow-through because they prefer to pursue inspiration rather than goals that require disciplined effort based on attention to details. They thrive on intensity. ENFPs are drawn to future possibilities, are good at solving problems, and are curious about people. They have many friends and acquaintances. Friendly, warm-hearted, and charming, they are concerned about the welfare of others and enjoy networking and putting people together. They can be idealistic and value self-exploration. Having fun is a priority. Because ENFPs dislike the repetitive effort that comes with follow-through and routines, they can become easily bored.

A strong system of values guides them. They prefer to present themselves authentically to others and seek meaning in what they do. They are easy-going, insightful, adaptable, persuasive, and can inspire. Independent, ENFPs are often leaders. They value being recognized for their authenticity and what they contribute to the welfare of others (Kiersey and Bates 1984).

Occupational preferences: ENFPs like work that involves people to people contact and uses their abilities to problem solve and generate ideas. They are attracted to professions that provide a variety of experiences and offer ongoing challenges for innovation. Careers in technology, education, psychology, acting, creative writing, journalism, health, social services, advertising, and business suit them. Professions that challenge their skills with people, problem solving, and generating possibilities interest them.

Challenges: ENFPs have difficulty with follow-through. They may leave projects unfinished after the challenge phase is over. They can have trouble disciplining themselves to do things they don't want to do. Since they are not impressed by authority, they may have difficulty following rules.

ENFPs can benefit from developing their weakest function, sensing, by paying attention to what is happening in the here and now, especially in everyday matters. Using the sensation function encourages attention to details like tending to the routine tasks of daily living—not losing things, paying bills, housekeeping, finishing projects. With this effort, their lives can be more productive and stress free.

GROUP THREE
The Introverted Sensate Types: ISTJ, ISTP, ISFJ, ISFP

GROUPS ONE and TWO examined the extraverted types—the extraverted sensate and the extraverted intuitive. GROUPS THREE and FOUR address the introverted types—the introverted sensate and the introverted intuitive. Here's the difference between extraverted and introverted sensates: the extraverted sensate experiences objects primarily as they are. The introverted sensate interprets objects as the individual experiences them from his or her particular inner perspective on outer reality.

ISTJ

ISTJs favor introversion, sensation, thinking, and judging preferences. Systematic, they like routines and pay attention to details and facts. They make up approximately eight percent of the population. Their strength is sensing, weakness intuition. ISTJs are loyal, responsible, reliable, hardworking people whose word is their bond. "Literal, precise and no-nonsense, they say what they mean and mean what they say" (Tieger and Barron-Tieger 2000, 84).

ISTJs organize their outer life around logical thinking that is based on their very individual inner way of processing outer sensory experiences. Their analysis, based on their own version of logical thinking, can be unique and unshakable. They are quiet, practical, logical, serious, cautious, accurate, thorough, and decisive in how they handle responsibilities. They like things simple and utilitarian and dislike extravagance. They pay careful attention to duty, are patient with details, and like things done their way. ISTJs value rules, hierarchy, traditions, and social responsibility. They compare present and past experiences in decision making and are dependable leaders. They work to achieve a result or produce a product and like to be recognized and appreciated for the results of their efforts (Kiersey and Bates 1986).

Occupational preferences: ISTJs are drawn to professions as executives, supervisors, professors, teachers, and accountants. They are suited to careers in banking, finance, business, and other jobs where reliability, attention to details, and a conservative attitude is of value.

Challenges: They may be inflexible, pessimistic, and reject anything that cannot be proven or is not factual. ISTJs resist considering or accepting what does not make sense to them according to their own thinking process. They may also have difficulty being emotionally available and supportive of others.

ISTJs can benefit from developing their weakest function, intuition. The skill of thinking intuitively is one of using the imagination to take in the overall picture, the patterns of connection that allow one to see beyond the details, facts, and the in-the-moment experience that the five senses present. By using their imaginations to consider intuitively perceived possibilities, they can expand and enrich their lives.

ISTP

ISTPs favor introversion, sensation, thinking, and perceiving preferences. They like action and responding at the spur of the moment. They are impatient with abstract theory or the intangible, and prefer the practical application of their skills. ISTPs are approximately seven percent of the population. Their strength is thinking, weakness feeling. "The ISTP nature is most easily seen in their mastery of tools of any kind..." (Keirsey and Bates 1984, 200).

Independent, self-sufficient, literal, precise, adaptable, and detached, ISTPs can seem distanced from others emotionally. They prefer to do things alone without the input of others, unless they are with people who think and act the way they do. They like challenges that test their skills, risks, and danger. They can turn to meet the moment and may be very capable of responding calmly, efficiently, and with a level head in an emergency (Tieger and Barron-Tieger 2000). ISTPs are process-oriented rather than results-oriented; that is, they enjoy doing something for the sake of doing it rather than the results to be achieved. They gain competency through doing what they love to do.

Their skillful use of tools and objects is the result of their ability to understand and organize underlying principles, facts, and data, and relate those principles to the concrete world. They like to figure out how things work. They are talented at the practical application of their skills rather than applying abstract theories and ideas. They do not like to be restrained, especially by rules, schedules, or authority that does not make sense to them or interferes with their lifestyles. They crave thrilling experiences through either work or play (Keirsey and Bates 2000). INTPs can be restless and dissatisfied with the status quo. "...they are loyal to their equals, they want no obligations, duties or confining promises, are uncomplicated in their desires and are trusting, receptive, generous" (Ibid, 203).

Occupational preferences: ISTPs are well adapted to the fields of applied and practical sciences and they are good at hands-on work. They are able to organize facts. This makes them well suited as economists, security analysts, engineers, or market and sales analysts in business and industry (Myers and Myers 1995). Because of their skill with tools and attraction to excitement, they can be very capable with weapons and effective in military and police work. This type does well in professions that deal with emergency situations that take advantage of their ability to respond to crises and use instruments precisely, such as fire fighting and medical work. They are also found as pilots, mountain climbers, racecar drivers, surgeons, and in other endeavors that push limits (Keirsey and Bates 2000).

Challenges: Because they rely on thinking to make decisions, they can overlook how they or others feel about what is being considered. They may be overly critical. Procrastination can be a problem. They may ignore authority, rules, routines and schedules. They do not like book learning that seems irrelevant to them, so may not do well in traditional school settings (Keirsey and Bates 1984).

ISTPs can benefit from developing their weakest function, feeling, to become more aware of their own feeling values and those of others and to allow those feelings to be more influential in how they conduct their lives.

ISFJ

ISFJs favor introversion, sensation, feeling, and judging preferences. They are devoted, considerate, organized, systematic, and concerned for the common good. ISFJs make up approximately eight percent of the population. Their strength is sensation, weakness intuition. "Here the primary desire is to be of service and minister to individual needs" (Keirsey and Bates 1984, 194).

Stable, quiet, reserved, patient, sympathetic, loyal, and cooperative, ISFJs seek harmony and like to help others. They value being useful, dependable, steadfast, nurturing, and compassionate and are well-suited to caring for home and family. Practical, traditional, realistic, and hardworking, they are also conscientious, cautious, thorough, and responsible. They prefer to follow a routine, pay careful attention to details, and be accurate, and they like life to be predictable. ISFJs may cling stubbornly to unique individual ideas that seem odd to others. They work to achieve a result and like to be recognized and appreciated for the results of their efforts (Kiersey and Bates 1984).

Occupational preferences: ISFJs do well in professions that provide services to others, require attention to details, and follow methods and routines. They excel in careers in education, social services, medicine, business, and others fields that suit their strengths.

Challenges: ISFJs may have difficulty with surprises, interruptions, and changes in routine. They may take things personally and have feelings that are easily hurt. They can become resentful of others because of their tendency to put others' needs ahead of their own in a way that is self-sacrificing. Because they avoid conflict, issues may remain unresolved. Their thinking and decision-making process is based on comparing past and present experiences, so they can have difficulty imagining how things will be in the future.

ISFJs can benefit from developing their weakest function, intuition. Developing intuition is the capacity to use the imagination to take in the overall picture, the patterns of connection that allow one to see beyond the details, facts, and present experience that the five senses present, and to visualize what can happen in the future.

ISFP

ISFPs favor introversion, sensation, feeling, and perceiving preferences. They are kind, sympathetic, down-to-earth, specific, and concrete.

They make up approximately six percent of the population. Their strength is feeling, weakness thinking.

ISFPs are drawn to the fine arts like music, dancing, painting, and literature. They "may be the most misunderstood of all types because they do not express themselves directly, but through action. Unless they can find a medium of expression through an art form, who they are can remain unexpressed" (Keirsey and Bates 1984, 204).

They are sensitive to others' needs and feelings, compassionate, and seek harmony. They are good at solving problems and getting others to work together cooperatively. ISFPs are deeply committed to family, friends, causes, and, as artists, to their work. They like to act on the spur-of-the-moment rather than make plans. Enjoying nature, excitement, simple pleasures, and privacy, they value freedom and action.

ISFPs are gentle, trusting, reserved, patient, and tolerant, but easily hurt. They may not be comfortable with expressing themselves verbally in either speech or writing. They are easy-going, generally optimistic, cheerful, and fun loving. Process-oriented rather than results-oriented, they enjoy doing something for the sake of doing it rather than for results to be achieved. For instance, the ISFP musician becomes proficient, not by seeking to achieve expertise, but by enjoying the process of playing the instrument.

Occupational preferences: They seek professions where they can express their artistic talents. ISFPs may become painters, sculptors, musicians, dancers, or athletes. As artisans and craftspeople, they like hands-on work related to sensory experience. They can be attracted to occupations in fields related to nature and animals as well.

Challenges: ISFPs may be overly sympathetic, become too involved in tending to others' needs, and have difficulty setting boundaries and saying "no." They may lack assertiveness skills and be overwhelmed by another's dominance. They can have difficulty with long-range planning and organization, and may not excel in school because they lack interest in developing verbal skills.

ISFPs can benefit from developing their weakest function, thinking. The use of thinking can balance their tendency to be overly emotional. By practicing coping skills like "Live in the Moment," "Don't Say 'Yes' When You Want to Say 'No,'" and "Detach," they can keep themselves on a more even keel emotionally.

GROUP FOUR
The Introverted Intuitive Types: INTJ, INTP, INFJ, INFP

Introverted *intuitive* types are intrigued by possibilities that are fueled by a focus upon inner awareness and imagery. Their intuitive process is directed inward toward the world of thoughts and ideas and the insights that can be gained from that perspective. Where the introverted *sensate* mulls things over in relation to how they interpret the application of physical objects to the outer world, the introverted intuitive is focused further inward, within the mind itself and what the mind itself can reveal. They are less attached to physical reality and pay less attention to what is going on in the outer world than the other types.

INTJ
INTJs favor introverted, intuitive, thinking, and judging preferences. They focus on abstract theory, logic, possibilities, and how to improve things. They are approximately two percent of the population. Their strength is intuition, weakness sensation. "Most INTJs are on a constant quest to increase their knowledge and, by extension, their overall competence" (Tieger and Barron-Tieger 2000, 44).

They value intelligence and competency in themselves and others. They focus on theoretical ideas and their application to the outer world. INTJs think globally rather than specifically and seek to understand the universe. They have a future focus that is energized by their interest in what is possible to achieve. They are talented at resolving complex, abstract, theoretical challenges that can be solved through creative insight.

Imaginative, hard-working, skilled at focus and concentration, INTJs like independence, privacy, and autonomy. They may be hard to get to know, have complex personalities, and be perfectionists. They seek right and useful actions and new challenges. INTJs can conform in situations that make sense to them, but not otherwise. They value recognition and appreciation of their competencies and ideas (Kiersey and Bates 1986).

Occupational preferences: They are drawn to careers that call for ideas and theories to be put into practical use: scientific research, executive action, social services, medicine, technology, construction, as philosophers, physicists, mathematicians, engineers, architects, and professors.

Challenges: INTJs can be easily irritated by rules and situations that make no sense to them, and condescending toward people who do not meet their expectations. They can be impatient and seem insensitive. Although they are emotionally vulnerable and easily hurt, they can distance themselves from others and neglect relationships. They may be impossibly demanding in their expectations of themselves and others. Also, INTJs can become so preoccupied with the inner world of ideas and possibilities that they are absent-minded.

INTJs can benefit by paying attention to what is happening in the here and now, and by developing their weakest function, sensation. Using the sensation function encourages attention to details like tending to the routine tasks of daily living—paying bills, housekeeping, finishing projects. With this effort, their lives can become more productive, stable, and stress free.

INTP

INTPs favor introverted, intuitive, thinking, and perceiving preferences. They are focused on the world of ideas and universal challenges. Intellectual, complex, and analytical, they have an inner absorption. INTPs are about two percent of the population. Their strength is thinking, weakness feeling. "INTPs are perhaps the most intellectually profound of all types" (Myers and Myers 1995, 90).

They are interested in intellectual pursuits and have a global perspective: "The world exists primarily to be understood" (Keirsey and Bates 1984, 186).

INTPs value competency in self and others, independence, and logic. They like to organize concepts and ideas, and are analytical, inwardly absorbed, and private. They may seem distant, detached, shy, impersonal toward others, and easily bored. They enjoy quiet pursuits like reading and research. Creative around perceiving possibilities, INTPs can become very preoccupied with their focus on the world of inner ideas. They are not interested in tending to mundane details. They choose not to dominate or control others. INTPs value recognition and appreciation of their competencies, capabilities, and ideas (Kiersey and Bates, 1986).

Occupational preferences: INTPs are good at generating ideas based on theoretical analysis; however, they are not as talented at implementing those ideas. They are suited to occupational fields that explore theory: mathematics, physics, science, philosophy, economics, psychology, teaching (in their preferred subjects), research, and other fields that require a high level of intellectual functioning based on logic.

Challenges: INTPs may be skeptical of anything that is not logical to them, and impatient with others or with what they may consider trivial. They can seem arrogant and condescending. They can have difficulty with relationships because they lack awareness of their own or another's feelings, and because they distance themselves from others through preoccupation with inner absorption. They keep their feelings to themselves. They can be irritated by and intolerant of self and others when their high personal standards are not met.

INTPs can benefit by developing their weakest function, feeling, to become more aware of their own feeling values and those of others. Allowing feelings to be more influential can improve how they conduct their lives.

INFJ

INFJs favor introverted, intuitive, feeling, and judging preferences. They are visionary, concerned with global issues, self-actualization, and the welfare of others. About two percent of the population is INFJ. Their strength is intuition, weakness sensation. "The two words that best describe most INFJs are integrity and originality" (Tieger and Barron-Tieger 2000, 52).

INFJs are independent original thinkers, creative and pioneering. They have a complex depth of personality. They follow values, inspirations, and strong moral and ethical standards. INFJs are insightful, perceptive, determined, focused, and may be driven to follow the call of the self. "'How can I become the person I really am?' asks the NF [intuitive feeler]" (Kiersey and Bates 1986, 59).

Sympathetic, supportive of others, patient, and empathic, INFJs can inspire. They are quiet people who seek harmony with others and self-realization from within. They are focused on future possibilities related to what can happen in the big picture. They are concerned about the care and welfare of family, humanity, and the earth. They like to be recognized and appreciated for their ideas and actions as they relate to the welfare of others (Kiersey and Bates 1986).

Occupational preferences: INFJs seek meaningful work in careers like teaching, social work, psychology, counseling, writing, the ministry, and as professors of sociology, philosophy, religion, and psychology.

INFJs are volunteers in their communities and throughout the world. They show up when disasters hit. They work in the Peace Corp, Volunteers of America, Doctors without Borders, the Red Cross, and other global organizations that serve humanity.

Challenges: INFJs may be judgmental of those with lower moral standards. They may have difficulty tending to the ordinary details of daily living. They can be absent-minded and lose things. They are easily hurt and have trouble setting boundaries and saying "no" to others.

INFJs can benefit from developing their weakest function, sensing. By paying attention to what is happening in the here and now, especially in everyday matters, they can function better day-to-day. Using the sensation function encourages attention to details like paying bills, housekeeping, and finishing tedious projects. With this effort, their lives can be more productive, stable, and stress-free.

INFP

INFPs favor introversion, intuition, feeling, and perceiving preferences. They are deeply caring, have a strong sense of integrity, and seek self-actualization. Approximately three percent of the population is INFP. Their strength is feeling, weakness thinking. "INFPs are on a lifelong quest for meaning and inner harmony. Their lead function is feeling, so they are driven by deeply felt personal values and are passionately committed to making sure their beliefs and actions are in balance" (Tieger and Barron-Tieger 2000, 55).

Idealistic, their focus is inward, reflective. They are very conscious of their need to act authentically, rather than follow the mainstream. They feel called to service. "To understand INFPs, their cause must be understood, for they are willing to make unusual sacrifices for someone or something believed in" (Kiersey and Bates 1986, 176).

INFPs seek meaning and inner/outer harmony based on strong values that relate to world harmony. Nurturing of others, sympathetic, and curious, they are nonjudgmental, loyal, and reserved. They enjoy the fine arts; solitary pursuits like reading, meditation, and journaling; and scholarly studies in philosophy, psychology, religion, and spirituality. They are adaptable except when called upon to go against their values. INFPs like to be recognized and appreciated for their contributions to the welfare of others through their ideas and actions (Kiersey and Bates 1986)

Occupational preferences: INFPs are attracted to professions that reflect their inner value systems. They choose careers as teachers, professors, psychologists, social workers, ministers, researchers, and serve in other fields that provide them with meaningful work. They can be found doing humanitarian work throughout the world.

Challenges: INFPs are easily hurt. They have difficulty saying "no" and setting boundaries. Regulating emotional involvement with others can be a problem. They can become bitter toward others because they hide resentments and avoid conflict. They don't like tending to daily routines and details.

INFPs can benefit from developing their weakest function, thinking. By using thinking they can balance their tendency to be overly emotional. By practicing coping skills that rely on conscious thinking, like "Live in the Moment," "Don't Say 'Yes' When You Want to Say 'No,'" and "Detach," they can keep themselves on a more even keel.

33 • Comparing and Contrasting Personality Type Interactions

Couples with different personality types, and their children, have problems getting along because people with different types think and act differently. Among family members, type differences can oppose each other and cause misunderstandings and conflict. By becoming aware of the type differences in your family, and compensating for them, relationships can improve.

There are 136 pairing combinations of typology preferences. Each pairing interacts in a unique way. The information presented here briefly touches upon the dynamics of these interactions. For a more complete account, see *Just Your Type* by Paul D. Tieger and Barbara Baron-Tieger.

Unfortunately, we are often attracted to a person with our opposite typology preference. There are two reasons for this. We admire others who do things well that we don't, and we intuitively seek to complete ourselves by finding a complementary partner. This attraction creates passion in the beginning, but often trouble later on. The different type combinations put more or less stress on the communication process depending on how many type traits the individuals share. None of the different ways of being in the world is right or wrong. Each is just different. That is why it is so important to learn how to communicate with others by listening with the authentic desire to understand, and to speak without making the other wrong.

After determining your own typology and that of your partner or child, you can find the pairing combination that best represents you and the other person in this chapter. In the previous chapter, the types were arranged into four parts according to the *first* two letters of each type abbreviation, ES, EN, IS and IN types. For comparing and contrasting purposes, in this chapter the pairings are divided differently—into ten categories. Each is organized by the two letters that fall in the *middle* of the type preference abbreviations rather than at the beginning.

For instance, suppose you are an ESTP and your partner is an ISFJ. Your middle letters are ST, and your partners are SF. When the personality types are organized according to the middle letters, there are ten possible categories. They are listed below. In the case of ESTP and ISFJ, look at number five on the list, sensate thinker with sensate feeler (ST-SF). This is where you will find the description of how ESTPs and ISFJs interact. Note that this combination shares only one typology preference—sensation. Because one person is an extraverted, thinking perceiver and the other an introverted, feeling judger, this pair may have trouble understanding each other and communicating.

Here are the ten groups of personality type combinations and their page numbers:

1. Sensate Thinker with Sensate Thinker (ST-ST), page 127.
2. Sensate Feeler with Sensate Feeler (SF-SF), page 128.
3. Intuitive Thinker with Intuitive Thinker (NT-NT), page 129.
4. Intuitive Feeler with Intuitive Feeler (NF-NF), page 130.
5. Sensate Thinker with Sensate Feeler (ST-SF), page 130.
6. Intuitive Thinker with Intuitive Feeler (NT-NF), page 131.
7. Sensate Thinker with Intuitive Thinker (ST-NT), page 132.
8. Sensate Feeler with Intuitive Feeler (SF-NF), page 133.
9. Sensate Thinker with Intuitive Feeler (ST-NF), page 134.
10. Sensate Feeler with Intuitive Thinker (SF-NT), page 135.

1. Sensate Thinker with Sensate Thinker (ST-ST)
10 Pair Combinations
ESTJ-ESTJ, ESTP-ESTP, ESTJ-ESTP, ESTJ-ISTJ, ESTJ-ISTP,
ESTP-ISTP, ESTP-ISTJ, ISTJ-ISTP, ISTJ-ISTJ, ISTP-ISTP.

When two sensate thinkers are communicating, they share common ways of acquiring information and reaching conclusions. Both depend primarily on their five senses to gain information and on logic for decision making.

If one is extraverted and the other introverted, they have different preferences for focusing the mind's attention, the extravert on the outer world of people and things, the introvert on the inner one of thoughts and ideas. The extravert likes social events and being with people. The introvert needs more time alone, is hesitant about being in new situations and uncomfortable in large groups.

If one prefers the judging function and one perceiving, they have different ways of approaching the day. Judgers like to make daily plans, meet deadlines, and complete tasks. They value work over play. Perceivers like to let the day unfold to see what happens. They resist making plans and like to be spontaneous. Perceivers value play over work and want to be free.

The most compatible pairs in this grouping are ESTJ-ESTJ, ESTP-ESTP, ISTJ-ISTJ, and ISTP-ISTP because they share all four typology preferences. The chances are good that the two people in these pairings can get along and communicate effectively. Next in compatibility are ESTJ-ESTP, ESTP-ISTP, ESTP-ISTJ, and ISTP-ISTJ because they share three typology preferences. The least compatible of the group are ISTJ-ESTP and ESTJ-ISTP because they share only two.

2. Sensate Feeler with Sensate Feeler (SF-SF)
10 Pair Combinations
ESFJ-ESFJ, ESFJ-ISFJ, ESFJ-ESFP, ESFJ-ISFP, ISFJ-ISFJ,
ISFJ-ESFP, ISFJ-ISFP, ESFP-ESFP, ESFP-ISFP, ISFP-ISFP

When two sensate feelers are communicating, they share common ways of acquiring information and reaching conclusions. Both depend primarily on their five senses to gain information and on feeling values for decision making.

If one is extraverted and the other introverted, they have different preferences for focusing the mind's attention, the extravert on the outer world of people and things, the introvert on the inner one of thoughts and ideas. The extravert likes social events and being with people. The introvert needs more time alone, is hesitant about being in new situations and uncomfortable in large groups.

If one prefers the judging function and one perceiving, they have different ways of approaching the day. Judgers like to make daily plans, meet deadlines, and complete tasks. They value work over play. Perceivers like to let the day unfold to see what happens. They resist making plans and like to be spontaneous. Perceivers value play over work and want to be free.

The most compatible pairs in this grouping are ESFJ-ESFJ, ISFJ-ISFJ, ESFP-ESFP, and ISFP-ISFP because they share all four typology preferences. The chances are good that the two people in these pairings can get along and communicate effectively. Next in compatibility are ESFJ-ESFP, ESFJ-ISFJ, ESFP-ISFP, and ISFP-ISFJ because they share three typology preferences. The least compatible of the group are ISFJ-ESFP and ESFJ-ISFP because they share only two.

3. Intuitive Thinker with Intuitive Thinker (NT-NT)
10 Pair Combinations
ENTJ-ENTJ, ENTJ-INTJ, ENTJ-ENTP, ENTJ-INTP, INTJ-INTJ,
INTJ-ENTP, INTJ-INTP, ENTP-ENTP, ENTP-INTP, INTP-INTP

When two intuitive thinkers are communicating, they share common ways of acquiring information and reaching conclusions. Both depend primarily on an intuitive process to inform themselves and on logic for decision making.

If one is extraverted and the other introverted, they have different preferences for focusing the mind's attention, the extravert on the outer world of people and things, the introvert on the inner one of thoughts and ideas. The extravert likes social events and being with people. The introvert needs more time alone, is hesitant about being in new situations and uncomfortable in large groups.

If one prefers the judging function and one perceiving, they have different ways of approaching the day. Judgers like to make daily plans, meet deadlines, and complete tasks. They value work over play. Perceivers like to let the day unfold to see what happens. They resist making plans and like to be spontaneous. Perceivers value play over work and want to be free.

The most compatible pairs in this grouping are ENTJ-ENTJ, INTJ-INTJ, ENTP-ENTP, and INTP-INTP because they share all four typology preferences. The chances are good that the two people in these pairings can get along and communicate effectively. Next in compatibility are ENTJ-ENTP, ENTJ-INTJ, ENTP-INTP, and INTP-INTJ because they share three typology preferences. The least compatible of the group are

INTP-ENTP and ENTJ-INTP because they share only two.

4. Intuitive Feeler with Intuitive Feeler (NF-NF)
10 Pair Combinations
ENFJ-ENFJ, ENFJ-INFJ, ENFJ-ENFP, ENFP-INFP, INFJ-INFJ,
INFJ-ENFP, INFP-INFP, ENFP-ENFP, ENFP-INFP, INFP-INFP

When two intuitive feelers are communicating, they share common ways of acquiring information and reaching conclusions. Both depend primarily on an intuitive process to inform themselves and on feeling values for decision making.

If one is extraverted and the other introverted, they have different preferences for focusing the mind's attention, the extravert on the outer world of people and things, the introvert on the inner one of thoughts and ideas. The extravert likes social events and being with people. The introvert needs more time alone, is hesitant about being in new situations and uncomfortable in large groups.

If one prefers the judging function and one perceiving, they have different ways of approaching the day. Judgers like to make daily plans, meet deadlines, and complete tasks. They value work over play. Perceivers like to let the day unfold to see what happens. They resist making plans and like to be spontaneous. Perceivers value play over work and want to be free.

The most compatible pairs in this grouping are ENFJ-ENFJ, INFJ-INFJ, ENFP-ENFP, and INFP-INFP because they share all four typology preferences. The chances are good that the two people in these pairings can get along and communicate effectively. Next in compatibility are ENFJ-ENFP, ENFJ-INFJ, ENFP-INFP, and INFP-INFJ because they share three typology preferences. The least compatible of the group are INFJ-ENFP and ENFJ-INFP because they share only two.

5. Sensate Thinker with Sensate Feeler (ST-SF)
16 Pair Combinations
ESTJ-ESFP, ESTJ-ISFJ, ESTJ-ESFP, ESTJ-ISFP, ISTJ-ESFJ, ISTJ-ISFJ,
ISTJ-ESFP,ISTP-ISFP, ESTP-ESFJ, ESTP-ISFJ, ESTP-ESFP, ESTP-ISFP,
ISTP-ESFJ, ISTP-ISFJ,ISTP-ESFP, ISTP-ISFP

When a sensate thinker and a sensate feeler are communicating, they share a common way of acquiring information. Both depend primarily on their five senses to inform themselves. However, they have different ways of reaching conclusions. The thinker depends on logic in decision making, the other on feeling values.

If one is extraverted and the other introverted, they have different preferences for focusing the mind's attention, the extravert on the outer world of people and things, the introvert on the inner one of thoughts and ideas. The extravert likes social events and being with people. The introvert needs more time alone, is hesitant about being in new situations and uncomfortable in large groups.

If one prefers the judging function and one perceiving, they have different ways of approaching the day. Judgers like to make daily plans, meet deadlines, and complete tasks. They value work over play. Perceivers like to let the day unfold to see what happens. They resist making plans and like to be spontaneous. Perceivers value play over work and want to be free.

The most compatible pairs in this grouping are ISTJ-ISFJ, ISTP-ISFP, ESTP-ESFP, and ESTJ-ESFJ because they share three typology preferences. Next in compatibility are ESTJ-ISFJ, ESTJ-ESFP, ISTJ-ISFP, ISTJ-ESFJ, ESTP-ESFJ, ESTP-ISFP, ISTP-ISFJ, and ISTP-ESFP because they share two typology preferences. The least compatible of the group are ESTJ-ISFP, ISTJ-ESFP, ESTP-ISFJ, and ISTP-ESFJ because they share only one.

6. Intuitive Thinker with Intuitive Feeler (NT-NF)
16 Pair Combinations
ENTJ-ENFJ, ENTJ-INFJ, ENTJ-ENFP, ENTJ-INFP, INTJ-ENFJ, INTJ-INFJ, INTJ-ENFP, INTJ-INFP, ENTP-ENFJ, ENTP-INFJ, ENTP-ENFP, ENTP-INFP, INTP-INFJ, INTP-ENFP, INTP-INFP, INTP-ENFJ

When an intuitive thinker and an intuitive feeler are communicating, they share a common way of acquiring information. Both depend primarily on an intuitive process to inform themselves. However, they have different ways of reaching conclusions. The thinker depends on logic in decision making, the other on feeling values.

If one is extraverted and the other introverted, they have different preferences for focusing the mind's attention, the extravert on the outer world of people and things, the introvert on the inner one of thoughts and ideas. The extravert likes social events and being with people. The introvert needs more time alone, is hesitant about being in new situations and uncomfortable in large groups.

If one prefers the judging function and one perceiving, they have different ways of approaching the day. Judgers like to make daily plans, meet deadlines, and complete tasks. They value work over play. Perceivers like to let the day unfold to see what happens. They resist making plans and like to be spontaneous. Perceivers value play over work and want to be free.

The most compatible pairs in this grouping are ENTJ-ENFJ, INTJ-INFJ, ENTP-ENFP, and INTP-INFP because they share three typology preferences. Next in compatibility are ENTJ-INFJ, ENTJ-ENFP, INTJ-ENFJ, INTJ-INFP, ENTP-ENFJ, ENTP-INFP, INTP-INFJ, and INTP-ENFP because they share two typology preferences. The least compatible of the group are ENTP-INFP, INTJ-ENFP, ENTP-INFJ, and INTP-ENFJ because they share only one.

7. Sensate Thinker with Intuitive Thinker (ST-NT)
16 Pair Combinations
ESTP-ENTJ, ESTJ-INTJ, ESTJ-ENTP, ESTJJ-INTP, ISTJ-ENTJ, ISTJ-INTJ, ISTJ-ENTP, ISTJ-INTP, ESTP-ENTJ, ESTP-INTJ, ESTP-ENTP, ESTP-ENTP, ISTP-ENTJ, ISTP-INTJ, ISTP-ENTP, ISTP-INTP.

When a sensate thinker and an intuitive thinker are communicating, they share a common way of reaching conclusions. Both rely on logic in decision making. However they have different ways of acquiring information. The sensate depends on the five senses to take in information. The intuitive relies on an interpretive process from within for experiencing the outer sensate world.

If one is extraverted and the other introverted, they have different preferences for focusing the mind's attention, the extravert on the outer world of people and things, the introvert on the inner one of thoughts and ideas. The extravert likes social events and being with people. The introvert needs more time alone, is hesitant about being in new situations and uncomfortable in large groups.

If one prefers the judging function and one perceiving, they have different ways of approaching the day. Judgers like to make daily plans, meet deadlines, and complete tasks. They value work over play. Perceivers like to let the day unfold to see what happens. They resist making plans and like to be spontaneous. Perceivers value play over work and want to be free.

The most compatible pairs in this grouping are ESTJ-ENTJ, ISTJ-INTJ, ESTP-ENTP, and ISTP-INTP because they share three typology preferences. Next in compatibility are ESTJ-INTJ, ESTJ-ENTP, ISTJ-INTP, ESTP-ENTJ, ESTP-ENTJ, ISTP-INTJ, and ISTP-ENTP because they share two typology preferences. Least compatible of the group are ESFJ-INFP, ISFJ-ENFP, ESFP-INFJ, and ISFJ-ENFJ because they share only one.

8. Sensate Feeler with Intuitive Feeler (SF-NF)
16 Pair Combinations
ESFJ-ENFJ, ESFJ-INFJ, ESFJ-ENFP, ESFJ-INFP, ISFJ-ENFJ, ISFJ-INFJ,
ISFJ-ENFP, ISFJ-INFP, ESFP-ENFJ, ESFP-INFJ, ESFP-ENFP,
ESFP-INFP, ISFP-ENFJ, ISFP-INFJ, ISFP-ENFP, ISFP-INFP

When a sensate feeler and an intuitive feeler are communicating, they share a common way of reaching conclusions. Both rely primarily on feeling values in decision making. However they have different ways of acquiring information. The sensate relies on the five senses to take in information. The intuitive depends on an interpretive process from within for experiencing the outer sensate world.

If one is extraverted and the other introverted, they have different preferences for focusing the mind's attention, the extravert on the outer world of people and things, the introvert on the inner one of thoughts and ideas. The extravert likes social events and being with people. The introvert needs more time alone, is hesitant about being in new situations and uncomfortable in large groups.

If one prefers the judging function and one perceiving, they have different ways of approaching the day. Judgers like to make daily plans, meet deadlines, and complete tasks. They value work over play. Perceivers like to let the day unfold to see what happens. They resist making plans and like to be spontaneous. Perceivers value play over work and want to be free.

The most compatible pairs in this grouping are ESFJ-ENFJ,

ISFJ-INFJ, ESFP-ENFP, and ISFP-INFP because they share three typology preferences. Next in compatibility are ESFJ-INFJ, ESFJ-ENFP, ISFJ-ENFJ, ISFJ-INFP, ESFJ-ENFJ, ESFP-INFP, ISFP-INFJ, and ISFP-ENFP because they share two. Least compatible of the group are ESTJ-INTP, ISTJ-ENTP, ESTP-INTJ, and ISTP-ENTJ because they share only one.

9. Sensate Thinker with Intuitive Feeler (ST-NF)
16 Pair Combinations
ESTJ-ENFJ, ESTJ-INFJ, ESTJ-ENFP, ESTJ-INFP, ISTJ-ENFJ, ISTJ-INFJ, ISTJ-ENFJ, ISTJ-INFP, ESTP-ENFJ, ESTP-INFJ, ESTP-ENFP, ESTP-INFP, ISTP-ENFJ, ISTP-INFJ, ISTP-ENFP, ISTP-INFP

When a sensate thinker and an intuitive feeler are communicating, they do not share a common way of taking in information. One prefers to use the five senses to gather information. The other depends primarily on an inner intuitive way of being informed. They do not reach conclusions the same way either. The thinker uses a logical approach. The feeler makes decisions based on feeling values.

If one is extraverted and the other introverted, they have different preferences for focusing the mind's attention, the extravert on the outer world of people and things, the introvert on the inner one of thoughts and ideas. The extravert likes social events and being with people. The introvert needs more time alone, is hesitant about being in new situations and uncomfortable in large groups.

If one prefers the judging function and one perceiving, they have different ways of approaching the day. Judgers like to make daily plans, meet deadlines, and complete tasks. They value work over play. Perceivers like to let the day unfold to see what happens. They resist making plans and like to be spontaneous. Perceivers value play over work and want to be free.

The most compatible pairs in this grouping are ESTJ-ENFJ, ISTJ-INFJ, ESTP-ENFP, and ISTP-INFP because they share two typology preferences. Next in compatibility are ESTJ-INFJ, ESTJ-ENFP, ISTJ-ENFJ, ISTJ-INFP, ESTP-ENFJ, ESTP-INFP, ISTP-INFJ, and ISTP-ENFP because they share one. Least compatible of the group are ESTJ-INFP, ISTJ-ENFP, ESTP-INFJ, and ISTP-ENFJ because they share no typology preferences.

10. Sensate Feeler with Intuitive Thinker (SF-NT)
16 pair Combinations
ESFJ-ENTJ, ESFJ-INTJ, ESFJ-ENTP, ESFJ-INTP, ISFJ-ENTJ, ISFJ-INTJ,
ISFJ-ENTP, ISFJ-INTP, ESFP-ENTJ, ESFP-INTJ, ESFP-ENTP,
ESFP-INTP, ISFP-ENTJ, ISFP-INTJ, ISFP-ENTP, ISFP-INTP

When a sensate feeler and an intuitive thinker are communicating, they do not share a common way of acquiring information. One prefers to use the five senses to gain information. The other depends on an inner intuitive way of being informed. They don't reach conclusions the same way either. The thinker uses a logical approach. The feeler makes decisions based on feeling values.

If one is extraverted and the other introverted, they have different preferences for focusing the mind's attention, the extravert on the outer world of people and things, the introvert on the inner one of thoughts and ideas. The extravert likes social events and being with people. The introvert needs more time alone, is hesitant about being in new situations and uncomfortable in large groups.

If one prefers the judging function and one perceiving, they have different ways of approaching the day. Judgers like to make daily plans, meet deadlines, and complete tasks. They value work over play. Perceivers like to let the day unfold to see what happens. They resist making plans and like to be spontaneous. Perceivers value play over work and want to be free.

The most compatible pairs in this grouping are ESFJ-ENTJ, ISFJ-INTJ, ESFP-ENTP, and ISFP-INTP because they share two typology preferences. Next in compatibility are ESFJ-INTJ, ESFJ-ENTP, ISFJ-ENTJ, ISFJ-INTP, ESFP-ENTJ, ESFP-INTP, ISFP-INTJ, and ISFP-ENFP because they share one. Least compatible of the group are ESTJ-INTP, ISFJ-ENTP, ESFP-INTJ, and ISFP-ENTJ because they share no typology preferences.

References

Beattie, Melody. *Codependent No More*. New York, NY: Harper and Row, 1987.

Clark, Lynn. *SOS Help for Emotions*. Bowling Green, KY: Parents Press, 1998.

Geary, David. *Male, Female: the Evolution of Human Sex Differences*. Washington, DC: American Psychological Association, 1998.

Gordon, Thomas. *Parent Effectiveness Training*. New York, NY: Three Rivers Press, 2000.

Guerin, David. *The Evaluation and Treatment of Marital Conflict*. New York, NY: Basic Books, 1987.

Katherine, Anna. *Boundaries*. New York, NY: Hazelden Publishing, 1991.

Kiersey, David and Bates, Marilyn. *Please Understand Me*. Del Mar, CA: Prometheus Nemesis Book Company, 1994.

Myers, Isabel Briggs with Myers, Peter B.. *Gifts Differing*. Mountain View, CA: Davies-Black Publishing, 1985.

Millman, Dan. *The Way of the Peaceful Warrior*. Novato, CA: New World Library, 2000.

Nichols, Michael P. and Schwartz, Richard C. *Family Therapy: Concepts and Methods*. London, UK: Allyn and Bacon, 1991.

Sharp, Daryl. *Personality Types*. Toronto, ON: Inner City Books, 1987.

Tieger, Paul C. and Barron-Tieger, Barbara. *Just Your Type*. New York, NY: Little Brown and Company, 2000.

Wolfe, Ernest S. *Treating the Self: Elements of Clinical Self Psychology*. New York, NY:Guilford Press, 1988.

Zimmerman, Jack and Coyle, Virginia. *The Way of Council*. Walton Manors, FL: Bramble Books, 1996.

Made in United States
Troutdale, OR
12/20/2024

26965690R00086